Knowing Your Schools

Knowing Your Schools

Controversial Issues That Further Special Interest Groups

Jim Dueck

ROWMAN & LITTLEFIELD
Lanham • Boulder • New York • London

Published by Rowman & Littlefield
An imprint of The Rowman & Littlefield Publishing Group, Inc.
4501 Forbes Boulevard, Suite 200, Lanham, Maryland 20706
www.rowman.com

86-90 Paul Street, London EC2A 4NE

Copyright © 2022 by Jim Dueck

All rights reserved. No part of this book may be reproduced in any form or by any electronic or mechanical means, including information storage and retrieval systems, without written permission from the publisher, except by a reviewer who may quote passages in a review.

British Library Cataloguing in Publication Information Available

Library of Congress Cataloging-in-Publication Data

Names: Dueck, Jim, 1946- author.
Title: Knowing your schools : controversial issues that further special interest groups / Jim Dueck.
Description: Lanham, Maryland : Rowman & Littlefield Publishers, 2021. | Includes bibliographical references.
Identifiers: LCCN 2021035462 (print) | LCCN 2021035463 (ebook) | ISBN 9781475860337 (cloth) | ISBN 9781475860344 (paperback) | ISBN 9781475860351 (ebook)
Subjects: LCSH: Educational accountability. | Education—Parent participation. | Teachers—Salaries, etc. | Students—Conduct of life. | Vacations. | School sports.
Classification: LCC LB2806.22 .D843 2021 (print) | LCC LB2806.22 (ebook) | DDC 371.14/4—dc23
LC record available at https://lccn.loc.gov/2021035462
LC ebook record available at https://lccn.loc.gov/2021035463

Contents

Preface vii

1. You May Be a Student's Parent 1
2. Birth-Month Projections 5
3. Accountability in Education 29
4. Job for Life Is a Wrong Practice 49
5. Standardized Tests Are an Unwelcome Messenger ... 63
6. The Males' Ship Is Listing Badly 81
7. Teacher Pay 91
8. Parents' Responsibility and Right 101
9. Democratizing Education 125
10. Schools Deal with the Sexual Revolution 139
11. Students' Cell Phones 145
12. Unfairness of Prolonged Summer Vacations 149
13. Coaches Are Not Evaluators 159

14	Disregarding Our Best and Brightest	175
15	COVID-19	189
References		193

Preface

Forty years as an educator have made me acutely aware of the plethora of issues percolating in today's education system. Service in the classroom, principal's office, superintendent's chair, and educational leadership for a Canadian province as assistant deputy minister provided practical perspectives from all levels within the school system.

The Auditor General's Office for British Columbia identified me as their "most accountable superintendent" in the province and sent a team to interview all stakeholder organizations in the district for the purpose of developing a list of "best practices." My program included financial incentives for schools for successfully improving student outcomes.

At the provincial level, school and district report cards were developed with stakeholders and introduced featuring a combination of both raw (i.e., relative to fixed standards) and gain (i.e., relative to past performance) scores. This effort was one of the first to measure improvement and provide an evaluation based on multiple levels of performance. The success of this initiative resulted in approximately fifty delegations from around the world seeking to learn how educational accountability can succeed. This model also provided a model for U.S. states in their fulfillment of the 2015 Every Student Succeeds Act.

These delegations included Governor Tim Pawlenty, later a candidate for the U.S. presidency who wanted to learn about pay for performance in education; office staff from the U.K. prime minister George Brown; and that country's minister of education, who subsequently requested a personal presentation on accountability in the House of Commons for his purpose of "infecting government bureaucrats."

Later, Linda Darling-Hammond, a well-known researcher and author in education and consultant for the U.S. Race to the Top, contacted Michael Fullan from Canada to identify someone to provide a presentation to aides in the White House, Congress, and Governors' Association particularly focused on accountability and common assessment. This presentation was followed by the Department of Education to assist in launching their Race to the Top initiative as sitting on the panel to select districts for piloting common assessment. Out of these activities came invitations to identify winners of the various grants associated with the Race to the Top program.

In retirement, my role as a consultant has allowed time for helping candidates in civic politics, writing editorials for newspapers, and writing nine books prior to this one. These books identify how accountability can be used successfully to improve education and I am pleased to see that California now uses a school/district report card similar to the one developed during my leadership role in Alberta.

This book, *Knowing Your Schools*, identifies many educational issues presenting some controversies for educators, parents, politicians, and the general public. Extensive research is provided to assist the reader's understanding of how these issues confound the public's understanding.

Chapter 1

You May Be a Student's Parent

Parenthood provides one of the most exciting yet life-changing periods in peoples' lives. Anticipating the actual birth was, by itself, a time filled with preparations as well as some trepidation that the delivery would proceed as planned. Fear of the unknown was natural because so many birthing processes could interrupt the normal sequence of events, while considerable pain could await the mother and worry by the father. Receiving information about the newborn's proper functioning of body parts was the critical diagnosis before taking their newborn away from constant care and professional help.

Establishing early routines surrounding sleep and eating functions necessitated a regimented set of practices frequently based on some identified guru's philosophy. Undoubtedly, these daily routines were constantly reviewed and discussed with family and friends to determine how these should be revised or altered. This stage of child rearing required daily, if not hourly, care and discipline or risk experiencing unfortunate consequences.

Your child's years after birth involved a host of training activities requiring persistent and consistent supervision. When to begin potty training is a major time-consuming event filled with many accidents and dashed hopes. Nothing short of jubilation occurred when this important developmental stage was successfully achieved. Spending personal time with an early toddler, whether convenient or not, was the critical commitment for ongoing success in child rearing.

These initial four years provide children with important skills such as talking, physical mobility, and eventually, the ABCs and 123s. A child's brain is like a sponge soaking in likes and dislikes as well as explorations for attracting attention, both good and bad. Each day provides events producing delight or worry with frequent reference to whichever child-rearing guides are available.

Undoubtedly, variations in the rate of maturation compared with siblings or other children are duly noted. Understanding that children develop at different rates is a valuable lesson learned in these early years. Unfortunately, the school system only partially understands this fact which will be further explained in chapter 2.

Age four, however, is a significant age for most young children's intellectual development. Martha Farah's research reported by Jha (2012) explains:

> An early childhood surrounded by books and educational toys will leave positive fingerprints on a person's brain well into their late teens, a two-decade-long research study has shown. Scientists found that the more mental stimulation a child gets around the age of four, the more developed the parts of their brains dedicated to language and cognition will be in the decades ahead.
>
> Farah's results showed that the development of the cortex in late teens was closely correlated with a child's cognitive stimulation at the age of four. All other factors including parental nurturance at all ages and cognitive stimulation at age eight—had no effect. Farah said her results were evidence for the existence of a sensitive period, early in a person's life, that determined the optimal development of the cortex. "It really does support the idea that those early years are especially influential." (N.p.)

Maximizing benefits associated with a child's fourth year of life is also referenced by Kris (2017). Quoting Suzanne Bouffard, "self-regulation—the ability to manage one's behavior and emotions in a given situation—is the most important skill to foster at this age" (n.p.). Kris explains further:

> Publicly funded pre-K programs enjoy broad public and political support, largely because of research suggesting that preschool graduates enjoy both short-term and long-term benefits, including improved academic and school readiness, higher graduation rates, and lower incarceration rates. (N.p.)

A similar conclusion presented by Ristic (2016) states:

Preschool is an opportunity for them to be in a structured setting with teachers and groups of children where they will learn to share and follow instructions, raise their hand when they want to ask a question, take turns, and share the teacher's attention. Every child should have this sort of group experience before they start school. (N.p.)

After these years of being the child's primary teacher, the moment arrives when parents are confronted by a critical decision regarding from who and where the next years of education will be. Many parents spend more time deciding where to shop for clothes or food but merely *default their child's education to their closest school.* Omitting consideration of alternative educational sources may provide a convenient solution; however, the plethora of information about school quality now available suggests there are benefits in shopping around. Simply stated, *all schools are not equal.*

Wise shoppers pay attention to the labels attached to food packaging. The list of nutrition facts provides critical information about calories, fat, cholesterol, sodium, carbohydrates, proteins, and vitamins, and these data provide guidance for maintaining a healthy lifestyle. Shoppers may move quickly through some aisles because the necessary research was already completed earlier, but observing some shoppers pondering through this information is a relatively common occurrence. Our point is that not all cans labeled "pork and beans" are the same and, perhaps, there may be better alternatives for the next meal.

Shopping for the most appropriate school should be a similarly thoughtful exercise as choosing your child's menu. Some educators and their representatives may counsel that a school is a school and a teacher is a teacher. The curriculum, they argue, is the same because states and provinces publish a common curriculum for all students in a grade or course. These requirements may vary from other regions in the country, but the political region expects curricular consistency.

Quality of educational services is not equally consistent, however. We cannot even guarantee that each classroom is led by a minimally competent teacher. The proclivity of administrators portraying all members of their staff as outstanding, caring professionals may win their favor, but seldom is this reality. Shopping for the right school or the right teacher requires thoughtful consideration of the available data.

This book provides readers with critical information for understanding educational issues and making smart choices whenever opportunities are available. Alas, the most significant issue in education—that is, children have different maturation rates—is not adequately addressed within our school system. The next chapter provides a brief, albeit in-depth, depiction of how many students are systematically disadvantaged by a school system deeply rutted and rooted in the past.

KEY POINTS

- Early stages of parenting contained many uncertainties.
- Parents are primarily responsible for the first four years.
- Mental stimulation around the age of four develops the parts of children's brains dedicated to language and cognition.
- Many parents merely default their child's education to their closest school.
- There is merit in shopping for the right school because not all schools are equal.

Chapter 2

Birth-Month Projections

Our school system suffers from an old-fashioned belief that a *twelve-month window* is the most effective organizational structure. School jurisdictions typically welcome students into grade one after the summer break in the year of their sixth birthday. Therefore, in this model, many children turn six years old *after* they begin grade one; however, some school districts rotate their registration from September to August ensuring that all students enter grade one after their sixth birthday. Reducing the number of pre-age six students beginning the K–12 system is welcomed; however, this chapter presents the need for an even bolder shift.

ALL ARE NOT READY TO LEARN

Associated with the concept of "grade" is the notion that all children are ready to begin their formal learning at approximately the same time. Therefore, most school systems in the world utilize an organizational rule assigning a common date for students qualifying to enter the school system, even though there could be a span of 365 days between the oldest and youngest students within the grade cohort. Even when school systems rotate their school year, the age range remains constant.

The research community has paid little attention to the impact on learning success associated with the *maturity of children* when they enroll, or the *span in age* of the twelve-month cohort. Both of these issues are significant factors in student achievement and would benefit from greater analysis and discussion. We will examine these neglected areas and clarify how the current rules result in disadvantage for a significant number of students. Once the data is exposed and the unfairness is demonstrated, rule makers will be challenged to make changes and provide a more equitable learning environment.

It is incomprehensible to think that the education system could purposely continue providing unfair situations to a nation's most valuable resource. However, when a rule remains unchallenged for so long—in this case, centuries—it is difficult to replace it with an alternative. Peter Senge, a renowned researcher on change, once commented in an informal setting that achieving change in education was more difficult than in any other profession. We can explain this in part by the fact that the *relatively low level of accountability in education* produces minimal pressure from stakeholders for change.

Another reason for minimal pressure to change is that issues often appear complex to a busy, preoccupied public, which is the case with the issue we are labeling as *relative-age-effect*. In February 2011, the *New York Times* wrote about the manner in which New York City's private and public schools introduced reading.

New York State mandates that public schools begin teaching reading almost from the first day of Kindergarten, but private schools have the latitude to establish their own curriculum. According to Nir (2014) of the *New York Times*, "Some of the most prestigious [private schools] choose not to teach reading until first grade or later. These schools' deliberate approach is causing friction" (n.p.).

What is this friction about and who is it between? According to Nir, a private school headmaster commented to the media that "parents who get anxious think that education is like a race and you've got to get running fast and, if you don't, you're going to fall behind and then you're going to lose the race" (n.p.). A headmaster in another private school demonstrated a differing perspective by indicating that staving off formal reading instruction in Kindergarten "stops the growth [of a child] and could make education a potentially stultifying experience" (n.p.).

These different perspectives about the optimal time to begin instruction in reading leave a superficially informed public confused, uncertain, and unwilling to crusade for change. Given that relative-age-effect issues are significantly more complex than the appropriate time to introduce reading, it is understandable that there has been little pressure to change the rules about twelve-month grade cohorts.

On the other side of the continent in California, educators and decision-makers were also grappling with the appropriate time to begin reading instruction. California, along with three other U.S. states, allowed children to begin Kindergarten in September in the year when their fifth birthday occurred as late as the following December. Argenti (2010) from the *San Francisco Gate* reported teachers believed that "children with fall birthdays are disproportionately recommended for intervention: extra reading instruction, summer school, private tutoring, retention, and even special education" (n.p.).

Once this divergence in learning became a recognized phenomenon in 2010, California rolled back the entrance date for kindergarten from January to September. Such action addressed part of the problem, but another *problem of a twelve-month spread in maturity remains*. In California's new system, October to December birth dates are simply now enrolled in the following calendar year to create a twelve-month span from October to September. Consequently, some students will continue in their struggle to keep pace. As long as there is a *single-date approach* to enrollment in a twelve-month period, there will always be a significant relative-age-effect problem.

The issue is not only the month in which babies are born but also the differences in maturity across the cohort. The negative consequences of the relative-age-effect arise from the fact that the cohort incudes children born over a twelve-month period and that they enter this cohort at *one point* in the calendar year. These two factors combine to create an intolerable environment of unfairness for our children.

KINDERGARTEN REDSHIRTING

Redshirting is a practice used by some parents when their child, usually boys, qualifies for kindergarten late in the registration window. Delaying entry for one year allows their child to be among the oldest in their cohort rather than youngest. Gonzalez (2016) quoted from a dissertation by Dr. Suzanne Jones, who evaluated fifty-five families with adolescent boys and with summer birthdays. Thirty parents chose to redshirt their sons back in kindergarten and, using a recognized Life Satisfaction Scale, Jones reported that *redshirted students showed significantly higher levels of life satisfaction than those who had not been redshirted.* The feelings described by subjects in the interviews offered substantial evidence that redshirted students were happy with the decision their parents made, and those who were not wished they had been. Although this was a small study, it suggests that parents who opt to redshirt their children may be setting them up for a generally more satisfying life later on. (N.p.)

Samuels (2017) undertook a more robust review of redshirting and, using a September 1 cutoff reported:

The researchers compared children who were born in August and therefore are newly turned 5 when school starts, to children who were born in September and start school when they are almost 6. The study focused only on children who were "naturally" old for the grade or young for the grade; children who were held out of school for a year were not a part of the overall analysis.

The difference in test scores between these "young" 5-year-olds and "old" 5-year-olds was about two-tenths of a standard deviation. That's equivalent to about 40 SAT points on a 1600-point scale, the researchers said, or about the same as the difference in one-year learning gains between having a very strong teacher as opposed to an average one, according to a 2010 study on teacher effectiveness. . . .

Researchers also used data in a large, unnamed Florida county to analyze longer-term effects. In contrast to some other studies, this analysis found that the impact of being older-for-grade does not fade out over time. For example, September-born children—those who are old-for-grade—are 2.1 percent more likely to attend college compared to their August-born classmates, 3.3 percent more likely to graduate from college, and 7.2 percent more likely to graduate from a competitive or selective college.

They are also 15.4 percent less likely to be incarcerated for juvenile crime before their 16th birthday. (N.p.)

DataBlog (2011), in the U.K., also reported extensive findings supporting delayed entry:

Researchers at the Institute for Fiscal Studies (IFS) . . . studied three data sets, which represent the records of 48,500 children and teenagers in England. They found children born in August were 20% less likely than their classmates born 11 months earlier, in September, to go to Russell Group universities—the top flight that includes Oxford and Cambridge. They were more likely to study vocational courses instead. . . .

Children born in September score, on average, 0.356 standard deviations (i.e. above average), while children born in August score, on average, -0.461 standard deviations (i.e. below average); children born in August thus score 0.817 standard deviations lower than children born in September.

Teachers rate 13.9% of children born in September as below average, while they rate 30% of children born in August as below average; this means that teachers are 16.1 percentage points more likely to rate August-born children as below average. (N.p.)

Redshirting remains a hotly contested issue with research also opposing this strategy. Orso (2018) reported:

A handful of studies show that while children who are redshirted experience academic and social advantages while in kindergarten, that can dissipate by middle school. Some researchers argue redshirting can harm children's development over the years if they aren't challenged enough, and others suggest it's actually the youngest kids who perform better academically over time. (N.p.)

We recognize that parents have valid reasons for their struggle in making the best decisions for their child; however, the school system is absolving its responsibility by forcing parents to make this decision. This chapter provides a solution sidestepping the problem and negating most parents from having to make a controversial choice.

THE DOMINANT RULE FOR BEGINNING SCHOOL

There are many rules, conventions, and practices in education that guide its delivery and influence the degree to which students experience success. One such convention, which decision-makers have codified generally into law in jurisdictions, is the *annual single-date entry system*. It has remained part of the education system's set of rules for generations.

This rule is so dominant that educators plan virtually every other process around it, and its impact is felt in many other institutions and industries. Classes of students are organized after the first few days of school and rarely reorganized unless there is a significant shift in population during the school year. Even the educational terms "school year" and "grade" are based on the annual, single-date entry. Virtually all students progress to the next grade on the anniversary of their first entry date which is usually September in the northern hemisphere.

There are two variations to the idea of a single-entry date that are noteworthy: the emergence of year-round education and the trend in the United States toward an August entry. This latter trend follows the same principles of the September entry but merely rotates the annual clock one month forward. Mandating that all students begin a new school year in September is so common in our society that September is almost as important for new beginnings after summer vacation as is the traditional "New Year" on January 1.

Anyone attempting to mess with the common idea that school begins around the beginning of September does so at their own peril. Change is seldom appreciated, much less supported. In this case, the collective memory is that every generation has dealt with the annual, single-date entry phenomenon and parents have "always" planned their life around the entry date and automatically done whatever was necessary to make sure that their child was present and ready for the first day of school.

Schools, too, are firmly entrenched in the single-entry ritual: class routines are established, administrators establish school routines around it, students form friendships with the entry in mind, and teachers organize their lesson plans with a substantial review of the previous year's forgotten learning in mind. The beginning of the new school year is actually the beginning of a new life.

The September 1st launch anticipates another idea, namely that the year is a literal year with a beginning and ending. So engrained is the understanding of school starting in September and ending in June, followed by a two-month break, that any other approach is inconceivable. Even when a school system is so bold as to innovate with the September entry, it does so within the conventional twelve-month protocol. Schools that start in August, rather than September, close in May rather than June. A two-month break follows and a twelve-month cycle begins again in August.

The recent advent of large-scale, standardized testing provides rule makers with a plethora of data demonstrating the ill-effect of one rule, as well as how it can be altered so that our children, who really are our nation's most valuable resource, do not have to be negatively impacted for life. The single-date entry system is one of these rules which will benefit from reconsideration.

Changing long-standing practice is difficult, and our natural tendency to embrace order and stability and to avoid turbulence and upset for those with privilege means that change does not come easily. *In the case of education, rule makers must courageously step forward to ensure that all children are treated fairly and equitably.* Without acts of courage where ignorance, privilege, and complacency are confronted, the status quo will remain the modus operandi to the detriment of students and society as a whole.

THE PRESSURE TO SUCCEED

Parents express great pride and pleasure when their child is able to print their own name, count to one hundred, repeat in order the letters of the alphabet, read through a particular reader, and so on. Teachers feel the subtle and not so subtle pressure of curricular expectations or standards that are identified as learning outcomes for students in the various grades. Children are not immune to the emotional effects of this focus on their intellectual development because they sense the pressure adults are feeling.

This pressure is not inconsequential. In fact, our society imposes a great deal of pressure on children to succeed intellectually: it is promoted as the most important key to future success. As a consequence of this expectation, a child's self-esteem is closely associated with academic success. For the child, this pressure for academic success has considerable impact on self-esteem. Expressions such as "success breeds success" and "self-fulfilled prophecy" are not simply clichés: they have meaning and import for children in classrooms and both are tied to the issue of relative-age-effect and annual, single-date entry.

Early success breeds confidence in a child, who will then feel able to attempt the learning challenges set out in a curriculum that is generally designed to have most students succeed. On the other hand, lack of success leads to self-doubt and self-imposed fear about tackling any new learning when failure seems probable. "I can't do this" soon becomes the student's mantra leading to negative thought patterns of self-doubt and inadequacy, especially in relationship to peers.

The emotional well-being of a child is absolutely critical because *only one in eight grade one students, who falls behind the peer group, is able to catch up later* (Juel et al. 2003). Therefore, success in grade one is so critical for the child's well-being that rule makers in our society must consider all options which have the promise of improving a child's rate of success. If, as educators and politicians are so fond of saying, "Children are our country's most valuable resource," are we really doing all we can to accommodate the nurturing of this resource?

Unfortunately, the answer is, "No!" A year to a grade one student represents 16 percent of their very brief lifetime. Substantial variances in intellectual development are readily apparent when two children sit in a classroom next to each other and the progress of one learner, who has lived approximately eighty months, is compared with another who has lived only sixty-eight months.

The school establishment will rise in righteous indignation at any suggestion that schools are competitive environments where students are compared to each other. Curriculum is written in such a way as to describe educational progress in terms of standards, not rank in a class. The child, however, does not understand this subtlety, nor do many parents. The child merely notices that their progress and success is not yet at the same level as others in the classroom. The result is negative self-esteem even though they are pursuing mastery of a standard. The parent, too, notices that a number of their child's peers have skills that their child does not have.

In grade one, the ability to read is an easily quantified skill that reflects individual progress. Teachers trained to assess students on a standard still find it "natural" and intuitive to compare students when differences are so apparent. Some teachers still "mark on the curve" where achievement relative to curricular standards is replaced with a focus on achievement relative to others in the class. Fortunately, the number of teachers using this assessment technique is decreasing as more school systems adopt curriculum standards.

The central issue here is that some of the variance in early student achievement is merely a representation of a child's maturity based on their birth date. If this variance is significant to the extent that lives are impacted by loss of self-esteem and confidence, the cause of the variance must be considered for reform. However, the impetus for such reform must demonstrate a compelling story based on intelligence rather than merely intuition or anecdotal evidence.

In a recent discussion with a university's Faculty of Education, a professor noted that the issue of relative-age-effect was not new and had been the topic of discussion in their university for some time. According to her, what was different now was that someone was finally bringing empirical evidence to the discussion. What had been anecdotal for many years was substantiated by a large data base and a representative sample which permits extrapolation to the population as a whole. Previously small, isolated studies inhibited generalizations to all our students and schools.

This chapter seeks to present such evidence that builds people's understanding of a significant concern regarding *fairness to students* and encourages constructive action. Parents, and their formal educational organizations, must embrace their opportunity to shift the school system toward a student-oriented approach. *This hope is important because we only get one opportunity with an age cohort of students.* In the world of primary and secondary education, a disregard for fairness is unconscionable.

BUT ALL LEARN IN SCHOOL

Every year students are expected to advance in accordance with a specified expectation in various curricular domains before they progress to the next level. This means there are many more expectations regarding universal participation in the intellectual domain, and with this expectation comes a complex array of compensatory programs and strategies to cope with variances in ability, motivation, and socioeconomic factors.

Parents accept that children differ from each other and that they mature at varying rates. Of course, experiences and learning in the school further accentuate inherent differences. This leads people to attribute variances in student achievement to nature and nurture. This latter influence is frequently subdivided into categories such as parenting and pedagogy, which describes the close relationship of school and home in the maturation process of the child.

Western societies have shied away from efforts to control processes in the natural domain that shape and form the individual. Manipulating people through some form of engineering is generally thought to be reprehensible. In the nurturing domain, controls are often seen as acceptable, even essential.

Grouping students into twelve-month categories for efficiency's sake is a case in point. The negative effects of this intervention are largely ignored because they are complex and not readily seen. Now, however, a large body of empirical data has brought to light the serious harm this social convention creates.

Within a grade of students, we found a wide range of achievement. For example, examining more than a quarter of a million students over a five-year period (2014–2018) using Alberta's provincial tests for grade nine students in reading, 16.74 percent achieved the *Standard of Excellence* or "A" rating. However, an average percentage of 13.88 students achieved *Below Acceptable Standard* or "fail." A significant spread in student achievement within a grade is evident.

Not well understood, however, is how a cohort of students actually enter a school year labeled with the same grade but with many variations in graded achievement. Gagne (2005) records, "Within most grade levels the range between the lowest and highest achievers exceeds the 8-year gap in knowledge between average 1st and 9th-grade students. Moreover, the achievement gap widens by about 145 percent between grades 1 and 9" (p. 64).

Now it is possible to understand the inappropriateness of "grades" as we have defined them for generations. When a student is designated as "grade three," too many assumptions automatically follow and predetermined decisions and actions result. Most notably, all children tagged as "grade three" frequently are considered to be in the same instructional space at the beginning of the school year and are expected to end up near the same instructional space at year end.

Even as recently as the 1950s, teaching guides identified the instructional content for teachers on a specific date in the school year. While our educational system has become much more sensitive to the pace and style of the individual student, there remains a lack of awareness of how assumptions about grade level disadvantage individual children. Therefore, the vast majority of students continue to progress through the system at the same pace without conscious, intentional thought of what this means to students with widely divergent maturity levels.

STUDENT ACHIEVEMENT BY BIRTH MONTH

Data from our extensive regional study reveals the significance of the relative-age-effect in an annual, single-date entry system on student achievement (see figure 2.1). If it is true that a "picture is worth a thousand words," then this picture should be a sufficient reason to challenge rule makers about continuing their current practices. The results of this carefully crafted and monitored study over a six-year period show a *steady drop in achievement in the April–December age groups*. It provides incontrovertible evidence that the majority of students are not maximizing their learning potential in the current *twelve-month* cohort system.

This figure shows language arts test results by way of mean achievement scores for all students in Alberta with a birthday in a particular month of the year. Students born in March have the highest test scores and results for subsequent months show a gradual, but statistically significant, decline. *Simply stated, older students' achievement is higher than that of younger ones.*

Whereas a small majority of our school districts have a school registration cutoff date of December 31, many school districts extended the cutoff to the end of the second February. They implemented this procedure in an effort to lure parents into enrolling children into their district. Their expectation was that once in a school, there was a likelihood of remaining within the district and *retaining this funding.*

As the bar graph reaches the right side of the chart, the achievement level of students born in the *second* January and February fits the pattern that younger students achieve at lower levels than older students. The test results for these *second* January and February birth month students make apparent the foolishness of school districts permitting children born in these months to enroll in school when they are as young as five and one-half years old. It is an unconscionable abuse of authority for leaders to admit groups of students into a class when it is known their chances of success are significantly reduced. Thankfully, *government eventually responded to this data and ended this form of malpractice.*

One of the interesting, consistent features of figure 2.1 is the success of students born in March. Based on the rest of the evidence, this is counter intuitive. Students born in March are not the oldest but they demonstrate the highest level of achievement. January and February birth month students are older but demonstrate a slightly lower level of achievement.

The tragedy within this graphic is that there were many students who started school in that *second* January or February, but were too immature to achieve success. They were subsequently retained for a year, and then wrote

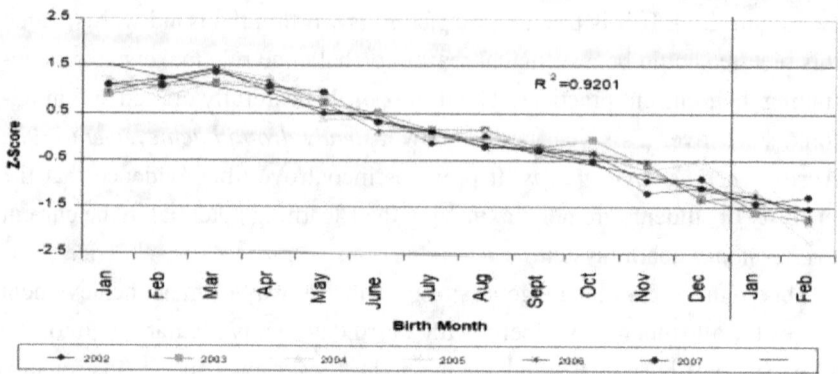

Figure 2.1 Grade 3 English Language Arts Test Results by Birth Year and Birth Month.

the grade three tests with the cohort of students born during the regular January–December registration period. The poor results for these students were sufficient to significantly downgrade results for students in the normal January and February cohort.

Even though these students spent an additional year in school and were *now with their age cohort,* their achievement on the test was not as high as that of their same-age peers who started school when they were six years old. In other words, the immature, retained learner pulled down the January and February results because the *damage to their self-esteem mitigated some of the success* they would have experienced had they waited to start school with their age cohort. In effect, the education system penalized these younger students and, recently, used these findings for abandoning this ill-conceived approach.

Success in life is not about performance in a one-off event but about a pattern of positive experiences that leads to a holistic health and well-being. One of the essential building blocks for such a life is a child's grade one experience. In choosing to minimize the significance of this, we are trifling with a principle that impacts children for the rest of their lives. When students wrote system tests in grade three, the age difference between students born in the first January and the second February was as great as fourteen months. Not surprisingly, many students born in the second January and February "fell off the bus" and ended up being retained.

The impact on their success in school even after being retained is so significant that when they did write the system tests, they actually brought down the first January and February achievement levels to below the success achieved by the March birth month students. If all school districts followed the same rule and utilized December 31 as the cutoff, the graph on student achievement by birth month would have been the highest for January.

The data in figure 2.1 yields additional information of note. First, the phenomenon is consistent across five consecutive years and *provides visual evidence that student achievement by grade three is related to birth month.* Such measurement precision is powerful and requires a thoughtful response from the rule makers on whether our education system is really operating in the best interests of all students.

Second, the data demonstrates the precision of these system tests as an instrument for measuring student achievement. The mathematics tests resulted in the same pattern of correlations and the same trend line. *This argues strongly for the reliability of these standardized tests, as they are able to assess analogous groups with analogous results.* Those suspicious of standardized testing find it difficult to explain away the overwhelming consistency demonstrated by such instruments.

Data for fourth-year students but in grade three is not included in this short summary. However, it reveals that students in their fourth year who were born in the second January and February period were still unable to achieve at the same level as their birth-month peers, in spite of being held back one year. The difficulty which began in grade one continued to unfold; once they fell behind, they remained behind and experienced an ongoing penalty imposed upon them by the system, not because they were less able, *but because they were younger.*

As previously stated, change is difficult especially when society has imposed a rule or convention for more than a century. Exposing a fallacy in the rule places considerable pressure on educational leaders, because ignoring the evidence really brings into question issues of motivation and conflict of interest. School administrators in this study readily admitted that this policy, which about 50 percent of the school districts adopted, *was based on financial considerations.*

In most communities, there were two publicly funded systems available which resulted in competition for enrollment. Many parents wanted their child to begin attending school as early as possible because of the no-cost, high-quality custodial care available in a regular school setting during the work day. The opportunity for free custodial care one year earlier than what was available with the other school district enticed some parents to select one district over the other. Convenience and economics were a higher priority than the child's best interests.

While school personnel are aware that intellectual development is a factor in student success, many parents lack the same degree of awareness. Furthermore, given the lack of a relevant data base on student achievement related to age-based cohorts, parental decisions about enrollment were based on intuition and anecdotal evidence.

In summary, the analysis of achievement data by birth month reveals how rules disadvantage a significant percentage of our students. At this point, it is appropriate to quip that an *important aspect of parenting is knowing when to become pregnant*. During a recent discussion of this issue with a group of parents, one mother responded to the provocative statement above by reminding everyone that "family planning" is an important aspect of cattle ranching.

While this was probably an attempt at humor, based on the idea that school boards should be at least as smart as cattle breeders, there is a sober philosophical point to be made: children are infinitely more valuable than cattle, so what are we doing creating obvious scenarios that lead to disadvantage and failure! It was as though she was saying, "This is something that we would never tolerate in any other realm of human endeavor, even the cattle industry."

Ranchers ensure that breeding is planned so that calves are not born in November when they have to survive Canada's hostile winters, but in the spring when they have several months to gain sufficient strength before the next winter season. "Family planning" is an important aspect of the beef industry. Indeed, a drive through ranch country in the month of May reveals herds of cows, bison, and horses with huge numbers of very young offspring.

In the school context with a January–December registration period, effective family planning suggests pregnancy in April for entry into the school system in January. A January birth month provides the typical North American child with significant advantage in two domains: the physical as demonstrated by Gladwell (2008) and the intellectual demonstrated here.

Gladwell's research uncovered the fact that there were a significantly disproportionate number of elite hockey athletes born in the first-half of their registration year. He drew his statistics from an examination of the roster of a junior hockey team whose players were aspiring to play professionally in the National Hockey League. What he discovered was that the roster of the junior team that he was studying totaled twenty-five players, fourteen of whom were born in the *first-quarter* of the registration year. Only six players were born in the *last six months* of the year even though this period of time was twice the number of months.

Gladwell went on to examine the rosters of all the teams in the Ontario Hockey League (OHL) and Western Hockey League (WHL). What he discovered was that there were more players born at the beginning of the calendar year than later. This pattern is not a rule because some exceptional athletes were born later in the year; however, the evidence was overwhelming.

During discussions with parent groups, reactions to these findings of both physical and intellectual success evoked interesting responses. Parents with children who were born in the first few months of the year beam with pride that they "did it right" and frequently react by giving "high fives" with other parents of similar good fortune. Presumably, they were merely the recipients of good fortune rather than the arbiters of good family planning.

One of the more interesting responses to this research came from a government bureaucrat who reviewed the birth-month data and said that it does not prove that older students achieve at higher levels than younger ones. His assertion was that students born in December simply may not be as intelligent as those born in January. After all, this could be a phenomenon similar to Astrology's "Signs of the Zodiac" which assigns to people characteristic variances depending on the time of year they were born.

This bureaucrat was frustrated by this relative-age-effect information because it had implications for leadership and, specifically, his leadership. Hopefully the observation was made in jest, but it was a challenge that required a thoughtful response because this research has not involved control groups. Therefore, like a crown prosecutor in a trial, circumstantial evidence had to be assembled to overcome his cynicism and guilt.

DUAL ENTRY PROVIDES THE BEST SOLUTION

A better option than forcing parents to consider redshirting is for school districts to implement a *dual-entry system*. Children born in the six-month window from March 1 to August 31 begin school at the beginning of September.

All students in this cohort would be six years old by their entry date in September. The next entry date would be for students born between September 1 and the end of the following February, who then would enter grade one on February 1.

In this second cohort, students born in February would commence grade one at five years and eleven months of age or older. This slight variation in ages between the two cohorts is necessitated by having ten months of school in a twelve-month calendar, where the summer vacation traditionally occurs in two consecutive months of July and August. Naturally, this could also be altered if a school system chose to utilize a year-round education program.

In this dual-entry model, each cohort would then be in school for five consecutive months and, with one birth month's exception, have children begin formal learning when they are six years of age instead of what happens now in many school systems where children as young as five years and eight months can begin school in grade one. The effect would be to have a four-month delay for the youngest students currently entering grade one. *Equally important is that the range in age of the students beginning grade one would only be six months and replace the annual single-date entry with its twelve-month age span.*

From an educational perspective, several major advantages occur with a dual-entry system. First, and probably foremost, the percentage of students achieving below grade level would be significantly reduced. Stated differently, there would be an immediate reduction in the percentage of failing students. Indeed, the reduction would be dramatic. *People find this concept difficult to comprehend because the reduction in student failure rates is so staggering.*

STUDENT RETENTION MAGNIFIES THE PROBLEM

Viewing the birth-month data for kindergarten in figure 2.2 beyond the month of May, we see a gradual increase in retention rates through the month of August before there is a steep incline that carries on to December and then an even steeper incline to February of the following year. Therefore, while the overall retention in kindergarten for the cohort was 2.9 percent, the rate for December birth month students was 15 percent and the second February students at 20 percent. Clearly teachers found that children born in the latter

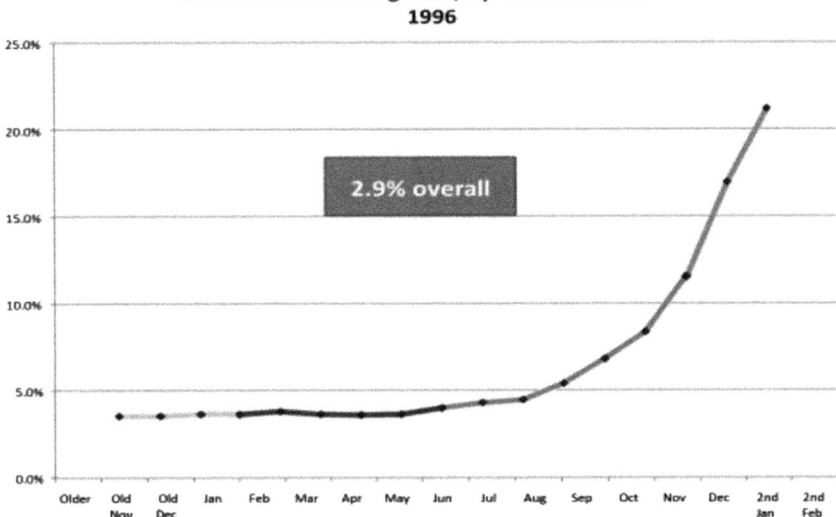

Figure 2.2 Percent Retained in Kindergarten by Month of Birth (1996).

portion of the registration year face a serious disadvantage and a greater need to be retained.

Figure 2.2 demonstrates a distressing illustration of an unfair situation with our nation's most valuable resource. At a time when social promotion was gaining prominence and retention was becoming an unpopular remedy for low achievement, school staff still retained a substantial percentage of students. The tragedy is that the vast majority of these retentions and all the concomitant social ramifications occurred with students born in the second half of the registration period. The story becomes more disturbing a year later.

When the same cohort of students completed grade one, schools retained an additional 2 percent of students across all birth months (see figure 2.3). Again, the retention rate was fairly flat from January through June before it increased sharply during the birth months in the latter half of the year. For the December birth month, another 10 percent of students were retained, and the second February birth month students had another 17 percent retention rate.

Examining the left side of figure 2.3, it is evident that some of the grade one students were already older than the grade one cohort group under investigation. Therefore, they were in their third year of school, counting kindergarten, and the system had already retained them twice.

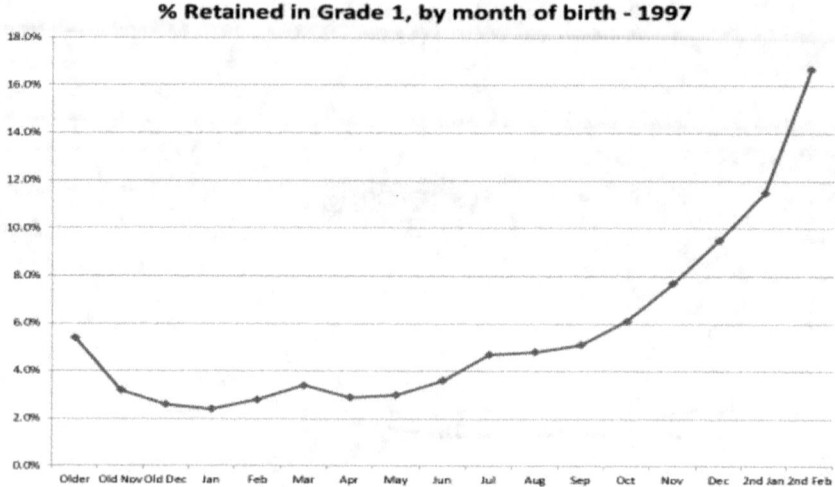

Figure 2.3   Percent Retained in Grade 1 by Month of Birth (1997).

Retention rates for the cohort increased in grade two. In schools that were still routinely retaining students, their modus operandi appears to have been to retain sooner rather than later. Nevertheless, they retained another 2.2 percent of the original student cohort with all months at more than 1 percent; the December birth month children experienced another 4 percent retention rate.

Again, these retentions only occurred in schools where the practice of retaining students was still employed. There were also many schools where the social promotion philosophy prevailed, and these students are not visible within the data even though they, too, would have been functioning below grade level. By the end of grade nine, more than 30 percent of the students were unable to pass the system mathematics test. From this, we are able to deduce that social promotion was every bit as prevalent as retention.

By the time the 1995–1996 kindergarten cohort of students left grade nine in 2006, the retention rate reached 13.8 percent of students participating in the formal learning program of grades one through nine (see figure 2.4). If the kindergarten students are added to the formal grades, the retention rate for all students entering the school system for *kindergarten through grade nine* was 16.7 percent or one in six students. December birth month retentions were almost three times the January ones.

In some respects, this data is staggering because many schools have a philosophical perspective that is opposed to student retention, and those students

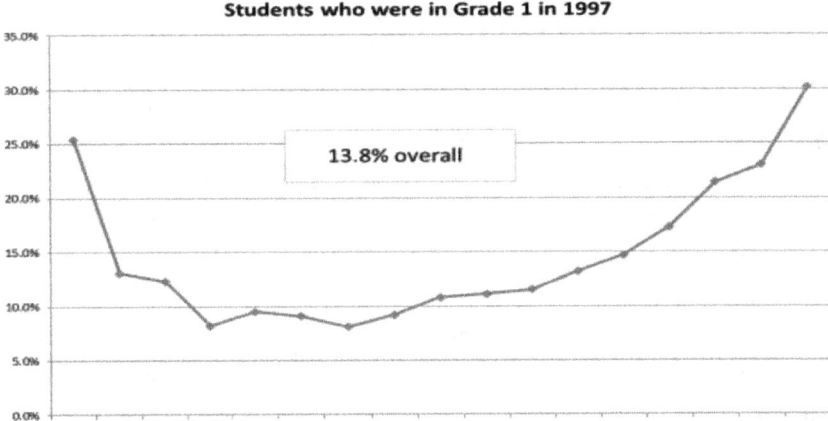

Figure 2.4 Cumulative Retention Grades 1–9 for Students in Grade 1 in 1997.

whom they socially promote are not included in the retentions. It bears repeating that this data represents only *actual retentions* because data on students proceeding as a result of social promotion was not collected.

Considerable controversy exists within the education community about retention and, hence, there is not a regional policy. Indeed, many school districts find this to be a contentious issue and delegate policies in this area to individual schools, so there is variation in practice even within school districts. Nevertheless, review of the data demonstrates clearly that students with birth months in the first half of the year are far less likely to be retained than those in the second half.

Explaining the data using actual numbers makes even more clear the size of the problem by giving students a number, if not a name. In the region under investigation, there were approximately 44,000 students in the cohort. Ten years later, 17 percent, or approximately 7,500 students had been retained at least once. Instead of taking ten years to progress through the K–9 system, these students took eleven or more years.

These retained students required considerable resources from the system. Based on an average class size of twenty students, an additional *three hundred and seventy-five classes were needed to accommodate the retained students*. The school system had to hire additional teachers for these classes, appoint more administrative support staff, allocate more classroom space, provide more custodial services, and likely build more schools.

Much of this added expense occurs unnecessarily and can be traced back to the negative impact of this relative-age-effect. Hence, not only is there a significant personal loss of self-esteem and a significant social loss of missed opportunity and contribution, but *there is also a substantial financial cost to the region's schools*. One is tempted to say that we could avoid all of this if the government and educators could convince parents to plan more carefully to have babies born in the first month of the schools' registration window. Alternatively, and realistically, these problems can and should be avoided by changing some simple, basic but unfair rules.

There are few rules in the education system that have a greater deleterious impact on students than single-date entry, twelve-month cohorts. How long will the unfair treatment of such a large percentage of the student population be tolerated before the public challenges the system to change? Once it happens it may not be pleasant. Until now, school systems have generally avoided malpractice suits, but the issue of bringing young students into an environment that predisposes them to failure, or at least to an unacceptably high risk of failing, has the aura of malpractice about it.

DUAL ENTRY IMPROVES STUDENT ACHIEVEMENT

It is possible to show the impact of a dual-entry system using data from the longitudinal study. Figure 2.5 depicts the number of grade three students who would have met the *Acceptable Standard*, if the school year was comprised of two entry points. Students born in the second-half of the current one-year cohort would be cut off from the bottom half of the line and would logically be expected to *mirror achievement levels of the first-half cohort*.

In other words, the September–February students would no longer be part of the downward slide after August, but will be on par with the beginning (March) of the continuum. Student achievement for the second-half of the school year would immediately improve by 5 percent, which is a significant amount for a school system. Furthermore, it would create an impressive savings for the taxpayer.

A significant benefit that might occur in a dual-entry approach pertains to the pace of student progress in classrooms across the education system. Intuitively it seems that teachers would be more willing to *accelerate* or *decelerate* students when there is only one-half of a year at issue rather than

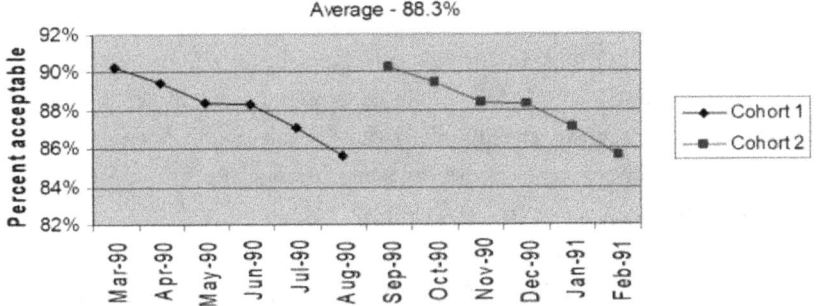

Figure 2.5 Language Arts Average Percent Acceptable by Birth Month in Dual Entry.

a full year. Dual entry does not eliminate entirely the "slave to the grade" mentality, but in the dual-entry system grades are replaced by levels where two levels equal one grade.

In essence, the elementary school program joins the high school system use of *semesters*. Grade one, for example, has 1A for students born in the first half of the year and 1B for the second half. When students in 1A progress to 1B at midyear, the students who turned six years old after 1A started, now begin their 1A program. Assuming normal progression, both groups graduate in complete twelve years with one group graduating in June and the younger group in December/January.

Recall that only 1 percent of students in our regional study were *accelerated*; yet, almost 17 percent were *retained* which, if applying a normal distribution, suggests that almost 16 percent more students might be capable of an accelerated program. *Accelerating students will be seen as a more viable option when the calendar year has two entry points into the school system.* The impact of a decision to alter the progression of a student by half a year is not as consequential as a similar decision that involves a full year.

Today, the lengthy summer vacation constitutes and communicates a clear ending to the school year. This lengthy break from formal learning contributes to an incorrect, public perception that students have reached a definite conclusion and a new beginning is soon to follow. Decades of practice has produced tradition and habit so that it is almost impossible to think of an elementary grade not beginning and ending for everyone, including the teacher, at the same time. Unless the school has a very small student population, they will not have the same teacher in September that they had when they "finished" in June.

In a dual-entry concept, June does not signal the end of a school year. Rather, it signals a break in formal learning time just like the traditional, albeit shorter, Christmas break. Usually, students remain with the same teacher when they return after the Christmas break. Students entering grade one in February could remain with the same teacher after the summer break concluded and when school re-commenced in September.

Few people believe there are "silver bullets" in education, but this has to be as close to one as there is. Saving taxpayers a large sum of money while significantly improving educational outcomes is unheralded! Again, this data is only applicable to actual retentions. If teachers did not also employ social promotion, the percent of struggling students currently traveling through our schools would certainly be higher. A dual-entry concept also alleviates parents from the pressure of planning their pregnancy for a first-month birth.

The data presented in this chapter would guarantee a huge savings or re-deployment of more than 5 percent of the annual operating budget while achieving a 5 percent improvement in student achievement for students born in the second half of the registration period. This latter point also results in a 60 percent reduction in student failure. Not calculated, at this point, is the gain in student success that would occur to our top achieving students, who would no longer be constrained in their intellectual development by teachers so focused on weak and failing students, which is their moral imperative.

Initiating change in education is one of the most difficult ventures because the opposite of courage is conformity. Hopefully, the evidence compiled in this chapter will provide sufficient courage to prompt rule makers toward a transformational change. Understanding how negative consequences affect both the oldest and youngest in a one-year cohort should drive policymakers toward a dual-entry program.

KEY POINTS

- Most schools organize around a cohort of students using a twelve-month window.
- A twelve-month age span in students creates significant issues.
- Relative-age-effect issues are significantly complex, making it difficult to

change the rules about twelve-month-grade cohorts.
- Redshirting is an attempt by kindergarten parents to allow students (mostly boys) to be the oldest in a grade.
- The annual single-date entry system remains a dominant concern in education.
- Standardized test results expose the unfairness of a single-date entry.
- Some of the variance in early student achievement is merely a representation of a child's maturity based on their birth date.
- Dual entry provides an educationally viable alternative with amazing potential.
- Accelerating bright students would become more viable with dual entry.

Chapter 3

Accountability in Education

The opposition to *change* recommended for education in the previous chapter is superseded only by the opposition educators have toward *accountability*. We examine this attitude as an issue with moral implications. Douglas Reeves (2000) stated it eloquently with the statement, "As a fundamental moral principle, no child in any school will be more accountable than the adults in the system. Similarly, it is a moral principle of leadership that no teacher or staff member will be more accountable than the leaders in the system" (n.p.).

Subsequent to Reeves' statement about no child being held to greater accountability than his or her teacher, Weber et al. (2009) also conducted a large-scale study on assessment with a similar conclusion; *in their mind, the teacher should be assessed more than the student*. These conclusions lead us into an interesting and provocative discussion.

STUDENTS ARE MORE ACCOUNTABLE THAN THEIR EDUCATORS

Since learning is so important in our culture, it is logical to expect that teacher evaluations will be based on how well their students achieve what is taught. Weisberg et al. (2009) summarize reality indicating that student academic progress rarely factors directly into evaluations. Teacher evaluations tend to focus on a teacher's behaviors and practices which may not have any impact on student learning such as the appearance of the classroom's bulletin boards. Essentially, teacher evaluations are virtually disconnected from their mandate, and *what doesn't seem to matter is what really matters: student achievement.*

Consider how *frequently* students are assessed, and compare this comprehensive schedule to the evaluation program for teachers. Students experience constant informal assessments on a *daily basis*; yet, too many teachers indicate that they seldom are evaluated and that their principal never enters their classroom. Even classroom monitoring is infrequent.

When students receive their report cards from teachers, they contain vastly different assessment information than what is provided to teachers. A student report card utilizes many categories of learning with *multiple areas of focus*. For example, evaluation is reported on progress in language arts which is broken into subcategories such as reading, listening, spelling, writing, and so on; a similar use of subcategories is followed within most other courses. The point is that students and their parents receive detailed assessments in *multiple areas* of their work.

These assessments are embellished by rating systems that seek to show the degree to which learning and skill development occurred. The practices of using letter grades (A, B, C, D, and F), percentages, or other coded symbols are fairly common methods for providing *greater precision* in evaluating student achievement. Some teachers even assign "+" or "–" values to letter grades which provides greater specificity. The point is that student learning is evaluated with a system using *multiple ratings* in *multiple aspects* of a course.

Similar scrutiny and precision are noticeably lacking in teacher evaluations where those doing the assessment typically use a binary approach for rating teachers as "satisfactory" or "unsatisfactory." While "unsatisfactory" is grounds for dismissal, it is rarely used in education. Using "satisfactory" fails to distinguish great teaching from good, and good from fair. The analysis by Weisberg et al. (2009) concluded that even when teacher evaluations require more than two ratings, the top rating is most frequent. *Essentially, teacher evaluations are meaningless because they do not differentiate talent or monitor degrees of success.*

Unlike student reports where subcategories of courses are also evaluated, teacher reports seldom, if ever, provide a rating of specific teaching elements. Comments pertaining to these elements may be provided but an actual proficiency rating seldom occurs. The assessment of the teacher's quality is, in essence, left up to the reader to glean from the written comments. Or, as some school district staff admitted, it is more important in reading teacher evaluation reports to look for what is *not* written. When specific teaching elements are silent in a report, it usually means that there is a weakness that the evaluator chooses not to put into writing.

Up to this point in our comparison between student and teacher accountability, the standard is clearly higher for students. *Reeves' moral principle is being violated*! In fact, the degree to which a double standard is evident is unconscionable. Politicians must be more demanding and teacher unions more forthcoming. Surely, the union's mandate for teacher welfare can be more than ensuring a job for life. Providing feedback to teachers on strengths and weaknesses in a transparent fashion can lead to a more fulfilling career.

There is a double standard evident between student and teacher when excellent performance is considered. Students' award ceremonies go well beyond accomplishments in skill-related programs such as sports and the arts. They recognize in many ways and in many venues how well students have achieved academically by providing information about high-grade point averages or letter grades. Information regarding scholarships is prominently displayed for public information, and excellence in student achievement is publicly celebrated.

This is not the case for teachers or for excellence in the classroom. Teachers may be celebrated for service outside of the classroom, but recognition based either on their performance evaluations or their success in improving student achievement is not. Yet, this is what they are hired to do. Where governments attempt to initiate such recognition, unions move to block the effort. Their unwillingness to recognize excellent teaching is yet another example of the double standard that exists in the education system which is constantly awarding excellence in students.

In our subsequent regional research study, principals were funded to participate in training for a "classroom walk through" program, whereby they would enter unannounced for a brief visit lasting but a few minutes. Their participation in this program included training in how to provide teachers with some meaningful feedback that would add value to their teaching. All participants across several school districts committed to *weekly classroom visitations with some feedback on observations for all teachers.*

At the program's conclusion, principals and teachers were surveyed regarding implementation and quality of feedback. Eighty-two percent of eighty-seven school-based administrators indicated that they visited only *three or fewer* classrooms per week. In other words, the principal's visitation program consisted of an average of zero to three classrooms per week.

These schools had many classrooms and most of the teachers surveyed indicated that their classroom was never visited despite the principals' commitment to undertake weekly visits. It is reasonable that many of these principals could be categorized among the enlightened ones, considering the commitment their jurisdictions demonstrated in promoting principal visibility in classrooms. If we were to look at the overall population of school administrators, the percentage of principals being absent from the classroom would be even higher.

This study is a sad commentary on the assessment that is going on in our schools: it is particularly sobering because it reflects poorly on the follow-through of school leaders who committed to an activity and received support through *training and special funding*. Equally disturbing was the lack of follow-through from district administrators who organized their district's participation and provided an advocacy role for this supervision model.

A typical grade one student in these schools was assessed daily in several subject areas and received four formal evaluation summaries during the year. These quarterly report cards included letter grades summarizing their achievement as well as effort; contained extensive written comments explaining these letter grades; assessed students in many subjects as well as components or subunits of subjects; focused on learning as well as effort, and culminated with a year-end indication whether performance was sufficient to move forward or pass. Such is the accountability of a grade one student, and such is the reporting process *every* school year thereafter.

Contrast these stringent procedures placed upon our student workers in the classroom with those evident in teacher evaluation. Sawchuck (2014) reported that by 2013, twenty-eight U.S. states had moved to require teachers to be evaluated annually, up from fifteen in 2009, and forty-one states required consideration of student-achievement data, up from fifteen in 2009.

While teacher evaluation expectations are increasing, the process is frequently circumvented when principals seek to avoid the discomfort of simply entering a classroom to observe teaching. Robinson (2018) reported how teachers can manipulate the supervision process:

Many teachers confess to putting on the "snapshot lesson," also known as the "dog-and-pony" show when the principal comes into the room. Principals may even hear multiple complaints about a teacher from parents, students, and colleagues over the course of a school year, but when they enter the classroom to conduct the observation, they find a well-managed class with a perfectly executed lesson in place. Couple this with a lack of specific, meaningful and actionable feedback from administrators and it leaves teachers feeling as if evaluation doesn't count for much outside of the summative rating they receive that puts their minds at ease (or perhaps causes undue stress) until the next cycle. (N.p.)

This approach to teacher supervision, which encourages canned lessons, is equally perverse with students submitting for marks a homework project completed by their parents. Teachers want to assess the competence and understanding demonstrated by students, and we should expect principals to assess teachers' competence without manipulation of the learning environment. Robinson also presents a 2018 report by the National Council on Teacher Quality describing case studies of successful teacher evaluation systems in school districts in six different states and a set of core principles responsible for their success:

- Multiple measures
- Student surveys
- Objective measures of student growth
- At least three rating categories
- Annual evaluations and observations for all teachers
- Professional development tied to evaluation
- Written feedback after each observation. (N.p.)

A controversial source of information for teacher evaluation is contained within this list of core principles. Client satisfaction surveys are a common measurement tool in business but are more controversial in education because students are the primary client of a teacher's service. Lafee (2014) summarizes a comprehensive study regarding the value of these surveys:

In 2009, the Bill & Melinda Gates Foundation funded a massive project called the Measures of Effective Teaching, or MET, which studied 3,000 volunteer teachers in seven cities. Among the project elements was a survey of tens of thousands of students asking them about their educational experiences, comparing those answers to test scores and other measures of teacher effectiveness. The MET researchers concluded that students were better than trained adult observers at evaluating teachers. Their perceptions clearly identified teacher strengths and areas for improvement, and reflected the values of the teacher. Equally important, student perceptions had predictive validity. They forecast with reliable consistency how students would fare on standardized tests and other measures of achievement. Published in September 2012, the MET study has strongly buttressed the push for student feedback. (N.p.)

As of 2020, only thirty-one U.S. states incorporate surveys about teacher performance.

Student academic growth data, as measured by standardized tests, is another controversial component in teacher evaluations. The website—https://www.nctq.org/pages/State-of-the-States-2019:-Teacher-and-Principal-Evaluation-Policy—reveals that twenty-five states moved forward with this requirement before 2015 and only one since 2015. While thirteen states never required this information, twelve had incorporated the requirement but subsequently retreated.

Finally, states are making progress in increasing educators' accountability by removing binary evaluations and incorporating levels of proficiency. Forty-one states have progressed to evaluations concluding with multiple levels of quality. This feature alone dispels the myth that a teacher is a teacher because not all teachers are equally talented and, therefore, not all schools are equally proficient.

Tyler and Tyler (2020) examined and quantified how teacher evaluation programs add value to student achievement:

> The achievement of individual teachers' students was compared before, during, and after the teacher's evaluation year. Their research proved that a student instructed by a given teacher *after* that teacher had been through the evaluation process scored approximately 11 percent of a standard deviation higher in math than a student taught by the same teacher *before* the teacher was evaluated. Ultimately, the research found that the effective use of the evaluation process developed skills and changed teacher behavior in a lasting manner, which increased student achievement over time. (N.p.)

Hanushek et al. (2019) went another direction by determining the effect on student learning using teachers' cognitive skills. Using the 2015 and 2018 worldwide PISA (Programme for International Student Assessment) test results, these researchers concluded:

> We find that teachers' cognitive skills differ widely among nations—and that these differences matter greatly for students' success in school. An increase of one standard deviation in teacher cognitive skills is associated with an increase of 10 to 15 percent of a standard deviation in student performance. This implies that as much as one quarter of the gaps in average student performance across the countries in our study would be closed if each of them were to raise their teachers' cognitive skills to the level of those in the highest-ranked country, Finland.
>
> We also investigate two explanations for why teachers in some countries are smarter than in others: differences in job opportunities for women and in teachers' salaries compared to those of other professions. We find that teachers have lower cognitive skills, on average, in countries with greater nonteaching job opportunities for women in high-skill occupations and where teaching pays relatively less than other professions. These findings have clear implications for policy debates here in the United States, where teachers earn some 20 percent less than comparable college graduates.
>
> Overall, we estimate that bringing teachers in each country to the Finnish level would reduce the dispersion of country-level PISA scores by about one quarter, reducing the standard deviation of scores from 29 to 22 points in math and from 22 to 16 points in reading.
>
> Improvements of this size may not be realistic in the short run for many countries, however. To match the cognitive skills of Finnish teachers, Turkey would have to draw its median teacher from the 97th percentile of the college numeracy distribution instead of the 53rd percentile. The U.S. would need to recruit its median math teacher from the 74th percentile instead of the current 47th percentile, and its median reading teacher from the 71st percentile instead of the 51st. (N.p.)

Barber and Mourshed (2007) in their earlier McKinsey Report alerted the U.S. education system about the lower quality of teaching candidates. They concluded that American teachers were largely from the *bottom third* of high school graduates going into college. Students entering the teaching profession are not the nation's top academic students, *yet they graduate from their training programs with the highest marks.*

The conclusion that American teachers are mostly from the bottom third of college students while graduating with the highest marks requires further clarification. Are these higher marks not evidence of higher ability for learning? Koedel (2011) demonstrated *how grade inflation is rampant in universities and how teachers come out of an education system where marks below "B" seldom occur and failure is virtually nonexistent.*

This analysis of major academic departments at universities demonstrates how education marks are skewed upward (see figure 3.1). Grade point averages for students enrolled in the Department of Education (cresting on the right side of the chart) were much higher than they were in any other department.

Therefore, aspiring teachers in their college programs received higher grade point averages than students in other programs, but this success was due more because of a greater propensity for grade inflation than academic capacity. Chapter 7 provides additional analysis of a teacher salary concern and how the United States might enable higher salaries for attracting a higher class of teaching talent.

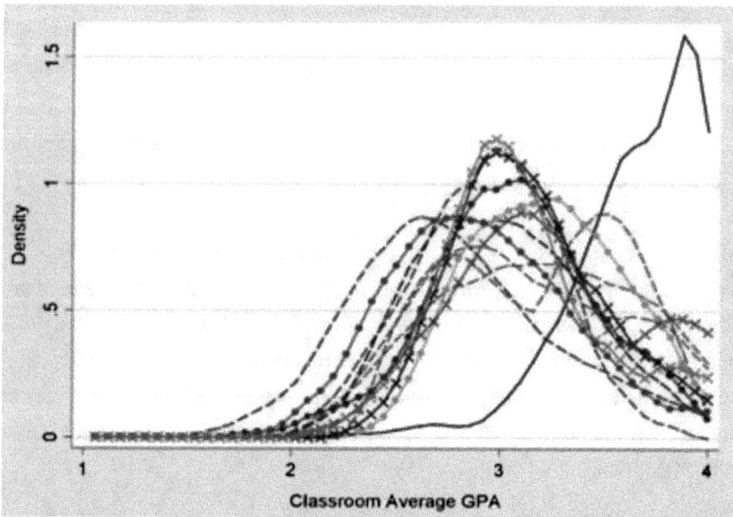

Figure 3.1 Distributions of classroom grades in the 2007–2008 school year for twelve major academic departments, plus the education department, for nonfreshman undergraduate classes at Indiana University-Bloomington.

SCORING THE WORK OF TEACHERS

Teachers are typically paid according to their university training and years of teaching experience. At some point, they reach their maximum on the scale and receive only cost-of-living increases thereafter. *Seldom is expertise taken into consideration.* In other words, within a specific category, a teacher is a teacher is a teacher. Until recently, quality of service is basically ignored.

This section examines a teacher-pay strategy known as the Tennessee Value-Added Assessment System (TVAAS) for assessing, or scoring, teacher's work in the classroom. William Sanders is credited with developing the system, first for Tennessee in the early 1990s and then later for a national clientele (http://www.shearonforschools.com/summary/GRAPH-SUM.HTML). This assessment program:

> Enables the tracking of the academic progress of every student in the state in the grades three though eight and beyond, as end of course testing in high school subject areas is implemented. The Tennessee Value-Added Assessment System (TVAAS) bases its estimates of the effectiveness of school districts, schools, and teachers on its massive, longitudinally merged database of Tennessee students' test data, which now contains in excess of five million records including two years of high school end of course results. (N.p.)

Table 3.1 provides mean scores for students in grade five mathematics in two Tennessee metropolitan school districts. Teachers for these students were evaluated in grades three, four, and five as being "low," "average," or "high," and were tested at the end of their grade five year. Mean scores were then determined for students who were with a low-performing teacher for three consecutive years (L/L/L) and combinations including average (A) through to working with a high-performing teacher for three consecutive years (H/H/H). These designations were based upon at least three years of data for each teacher.

Table 3.1 Cumulative Effects of Teacher Sequence on 5th Grade Math Scores for Two Metropolitan School Districts.

System	L/L/L	L/L/A	L/L/H	A/A/L	A/A/A	A/A/H	H/H/H
1	44	63	83	61	80	92	96
2	29	40	59	39	50	70	83

This table justifies the following conclusions:

(1) There is a consistent pattern of results between the two school systems.
(2) Three consecutive years with a *low*-performing teacher produced the lowest mean scores.
(3) Three consecutive years with a *high*-performing teacher produced the highest mean scores.
(4) The difference between mean scores with L/L/L in system 1 is 52 and in system 2 is 54.
(5) Student scores can be positively affected by the influence of even one average or highly effective teacher and that the same students will be negatively impacted by even one ineffective teacher.

Information truly is power! Parents privy to this information will certainly monitor which teacher will be teaching their child. School principals will know which teachers require their immediate attention. School district officials will know which building principals are providing effective leadership in staff development.

Feedback on performance is also powerful because recipients of information regarding their performance experience pressure to produce in the future. Such pressure is readily evident in the private sector where a bottom line of profit and loss on the balance sheet produces regular feedback on performance. In the public sector, this form of accountability is seldom evident. Quantifiable feedback on students' achievement will introduce this dynamic.

Assuming a low-performing teacher teaches 25 students a year over the course of a 35-year career, 875 students will receive a substandard education. This inferior level of schooling cannot be tolerated, and we must insist that both the teacher and supervisor are held accountable.

Of course, the proof is in the pudding, and we must see improved test results for Tennessee students on the U.S. NAEP tests. Results are available at the website—https://www.nagb.gov/content/nagb/assets/documents/publications/achievement/Tennessee%20Narrative%206.8_508%20compliant.pdf (P4). Between 2011 and 2015, Tennessee students went from:

- 46th in the country to 23rd in fourth-grade math
- 44th in eighth-grade math to 37th and
- 41st in eighth-grade reading to 29th

These improved results present a compelling rationale for other states and provinces to consider the TVAAS model. Unfortunately, not everyone in Tennessee is enthusiastic about the success and there are efforts to derail the program.

TVAAS scores include a $5,000 bonus for individual teachers and the potential of a $2,000 bonus for every teacher in the school if the school receives a high overall TVAAS score. Teachers' overall evaluations place 35 percent emphasis on TVAAS and the remainder on the principal's observations in the classroom. In 2011, the state sought to incorporate TVAAS into its teacher licensure process; however, the Tennessee Education Association (TEA) used the legal system to challenge this attempt in 2013. The TEA's position can be summarized as follows (https://www.nashvillescene.com/news/article/13049524/teachers-union-tvaas-is-a-bad-way-to-evaluate-teachers):

> In a last ditch effort to convince the State Board of Education to slow down its decision on whether to rest teacher license renewal decisions on student growth data, the Tennessee Education Association today is taking aim at the state's chief measuring stick.
>
> The state's largest teachers union argued to reporters Wednesday that the Tennessee Value-Added Assessment System, aka TVAAS, is an unreliable estimate of student and teacher performance subject to all the quirks of calculating statistics. Further, they said, it would leave good teachers without licenses. (N.p.)

Tatter (2016) at https://tn.chalkbeat.org/2016/2/19/21100522/federal-judge-dismisses-tea-lawsuit-challenging-tvaas-in-teacher-bonuses summarized the court's ruling:

> "While it may be a blunt tool, a rational policymaker could conclude that TVAAS is 'capable of measuring some marginal impact that teachers can have on their own students,'" wrote Judge Harry S. Mattice Jr. in his ruling. "This is all the Constitution requires." (N.p.)

This brief, but important section, is included despite the limited efforts across North America to incorporate teachers' classroom results into discussions about remuneration. Skeptics may confuse this effort as a strategy for getting people to work harder which, in some instances, may be necessary.

On the other hand, we can support this strategy as a means for getting people to work smarter. This strategy is not new because teacher professional development programs are operating everywhere.

Many school systems shut down for several days during the school year when children may not attend in order to enhance teacher skills in their classrooms. One superintendent made routine visits to schools and classrooms following a major attempt to introduce effective group work strategies in the classroom. Considerable funding for professional development was set aside, and several professional development days were identified to learn the process. However, during hundreds of classroom visits in the next two years, this superintendent never observed this strategy in use. If the professional development was useful, surely there would have been some evidence in the classroom.

The point is that we can show people how to work smarter but, for some, pressure may be required for them to incorporate smarter work into their classroom. We know that money works because teachers will invest time and energy to acquire a university degree to achieve another level in the pay grid. School system rewards this effort because of the belief that additional training and more information related to the profession will translate into better practice in classrooms. TVAAS broke the long-standing, ineffectual model by rewarding teachers based on their results in the classroom. It is now the premiere effort using a reward system during our six-decade review.

Politics play an ever-increasing role in education, and having one political party be more associated with educators is now the norm. We can look back at the introduction of Common Core a decade ago to see that politicians and teachers as well as both U.S. political parties initially supported the concept. However, when it was discovered that identifying a common set of outcomes across states could also result in a common definition of excellence across states, the alarm bells began to ring. It was soon obvious that performance pay was imminent, and this was something teachers and their unions found threatening. The resulting discord, said Russo (2015), threatened the entire project:

> Concern that the AFT, and to some degree the NEA, was flip-flopping on the Common Core, which could encourage classroom teachers' resistance to the changes and endanger the effort's ultimate success, has become a common one among standards supporters and union critics.

"It seemed like they signed on to do this [Common Core development] three years ago, banging the door down saying they needed to be part of it, and then little by little they've peeled off," says Democrats for Education Reform's Charlie Barone.

According to this line of reasoning, the unions expressed their support for the standards during the early stages, when they were being developed and then adopted by states during competition for Race to the Top funds. It was only when the development of assessments began, and the U.S. Department of Education's (ED's) No Child Left Behind waiver process included clear requirements for evaluating teachers based partly on student test scores, that the unions began to balk. (N.p.)

Not long thereafter, democrats, traditional supporters of unions, dropped their endorsement as did many republicans, who ignored the fact that forty-six governors requested this initiative, but incorrectly described this as a common *curriculum* and labeled this comprehensive improvement effort as overreach by the federal government. In 2020, forty-one states remained in the initiative but expressions of support from the political parties is lacking.

STATE, PROVINCE, AND SCHOOL DISTRICT EVALUATIONS

In 2008, the U.S. government's Race to the Top initiative convened a symposium about requiring states to prepare report cards on their education systems' performance. A Canadian province, Alberta, had launched its version in 2006 and was invited to demonstrate their model to various groups in Washington, DC. Alberta's model perceived strength was its focus on both *achievement* relative to defined standards and its capacity to measure *improvement* over time. Figure 3.2 demonstrates the five-point scale for each of these designations including the color coding (in brackets) associated with each degree of performance.

After assessing these two variables, the overall evaluation is determined from their point of intersection. For example, using figure 3.3 above, "achievement" at the "intermediate" level and "improvement" at the "maintained" level would be rated as "acceptable." The color coding for this overall evaluation is "excellent" @ blue, "good" @ green, "acceptable" @ yellow,

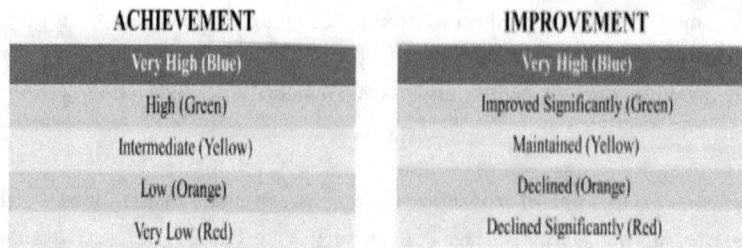

Figure 3.2 Color Coding Scale for Achievement and Improvement.

Overall Evaluation

▼ How each measure's overall evaluation is determined

Improvement	Achievement				
	Very High	High	Intermediate	Low	Very Low
Improved Significantly	Excellent	Good	Good	Good	Acceptable
Improved	Excellent	Good	Good	Acceptable	Issue
Maintained	Excellent	Good	Acceptable	Issue	Issue
Declined	Good	Acceptable	Issue	Issue	Concern
Declined Signficantly	Acceptable	Issue	Issue	Concern	Concern

Figure 3.3 Overall Evaluation Combining Achievement and Improvement.

"issue" @ orange, and "concern" @ red. This color coding allows readers to determine overall performance at a glance.

Readers are then able to view performance overall for the school, district, state/province. The overall summary above (figure 3.4) is difficult to present on a page but a version can be viewed at https://open.alberta.ca/dataset/7ebacc1e-cac7-49de-9a67-cd1f8e364a6d/resource/ce557447-1697-4f84-8f47-9557f028ef30/download/edc-accountability-pillar-summary-3-year-plan-2020-05.pdf.

Coincidentally, the State of California adopted a similar approach with their scorecard using a dashboard indicator as identified in figure 3.5 and also uses five colors to score measures in their school system.

Performance assessment within the school system has a long history for the clients, our students, and is finally progressing for both the efforts of educators as well as their educational organizations. Considerably, more must be accomplished regarding accountability or consequences before we can acknowledge that education workers are equally accountable as their clients, our students.

Provincial Accountability Pillar Overall Summary
October 2009

Government of Alberta ■ Education

Goal	Measure Category	Measure Category Evaluation	Measure	Alberta Current Result	Alberta Prev. Year Result	Alberta Prev. 3 Year Average	Measure Evaluation Achievement	Measure Evaluation Improvement	Measure Evaluation Overall
Goal 1: High Quality Learning Opportunities for All	Safe and Caring Schools	Good	Safe and Caring	86.9	85.1	84.6	High	Improved Significantly	Good
	Student Learning Opportunities	Good	Program of Studies	80.3	79.4	78.7	High	Improved Significantly	Good
			Education Quality	89.3	88.2	87.8	High	Improved Significantly	Good
			Dropout Rate	4.8	5.0	4.9	Intermediate	Maintained	Acceptable
			High School Completion Rate (3 yr)	70.7	71.0	70.6	Intermediate	Maintained	Acceptable
Goal 2: Excellence in Learner Outcomes	Student Learning Achievement (Grades K–9)	Good	PAT: Acceptable	76.8	75.3	75.6	Intermediate	Improved Significantly	Good
			PAT: Excellence	19.2	18.3	18.3	High	Improved Significantly	Good
	Student Learning Achievement (Grades 10–12)	n/a	Diploma: Acceptable	84.4	84.4	84.5	Intermediate	Maintained	Acceptable
			Diploma: Excellence	19.1	19.4	20.3	Intermediate	Declined Significantly	Issue
			Diploma Exam Participation Rate (4+ Exams)	53.3	53.6	53.6	Intermediate	Maintained	Acceptable
			Rutherford Scholarship	57.3	56.8	55.8	Intermediate	n/a	n/a
	Preparation for Lifelong Learning, World of Work, Citizenship	Good	Transition Rate (6 yr)	60.7	60.3	59.1	High	Improved Significantly	Good
			Work Preparation	79.6	80.1	78.1	High	Improved Significantly	Good
			Citizenship	80.3	77.9	77.1	High	Improved Significantly	Good
Goal 3: Highly Responsive and Responsible Ministry	Parental Involvement	Good	Parental Involvement	80.1	78.2	77.9	High	Improved Significantly	Good
	Continuous Improvement	Good	School Improvement	79.4	77.0	76.7	High	Improved Significantly	Good

Figure 3.4 Overall Summary Scorecard.

Figure 3.5   California Dashboard (Red, Orange, Yellow, Green, and Blue).

ACCOUNTABILITY REQUIRES CONSEQUENCES

The word "accountability" is one of the most frequently used words in political speeches. Rhetoric is cheap but action requires a plan because *accountability without consequences is not accountability.* We can only claim accountability is rendered when consequences—positive or negative—follow performance appraisals. Terminated employment, demotion, and fines are common forms of negative consequences; however, there must be additional strategies beyond promotion and "happy face notes" for positive consequences.

Financial remuneration (e.g., bonuses) provides employees with positive consequences for demonstrated success. This chapter identifies how we can measure teacher and school success and, when high levels of performance are achieved, these should be rewarded. Teachers' unions regard this notion with considerable animosity because they fear that their members will feel pressure to improve performance. Comparison is one of the ugliest concepts in education, and teachers react negatively toward assessments of their performance while assessing their students.

Team awards are a more palatable and logical solution for recognizing superior performance. Rarely is an individual teacher entirely responsible for a student's success. Schools can be a team venture similar to what is evident in business. Student success rather than profit is the bottom line!

Education can incorporate performance incentives using their school and district report cards to assess team performance, whether it be for groups or entire staff.

School systems such as districts can employ a similar approach with their employees' leadership. Unions are an adversarial special interest group seeking to improve the fortunes of their members; yet, they ardently want to be considered as educational partners. A partnership with government—which leads and allocates funds—and with parents—who are the system's clients—and the public—who pays the bills—is conceivable. Partners share in the good and the bad. In this partnership, consequences are applied based on performance recorded on the school system's report card.

Creativity may be necessary to operationalize such a new approach. For example, at the conclusion of the annual reporting cycle, the school district could send the union a financial reward commensurate with the district's report card when various degrees of improved outcomes are achieved. Union management would determine disposition of this incentive award.

There is a second component to this educational partnership. Political leadership should be removed when system results are not improving and a similar consequence should be applied to the partners providing leadership to teachers. Just as political leadership can be "punted" when the school system fails to deliver quality educational services, so should the partner's leadership be removed.

Government legislation should be in place quantifying superior or a failed report card incorporating both positive recognition as well as principles of progressive discipline beginning with "letters of warning." Applying "smart" pressure by way of a group reward is one way to incentivize the system. Bonus pay, funding for additional professional development, public recognition, and letters of commendation are examples of positive consequences.

Our initiative with system report cards included applying consequences for poor performance. Three Alberta school districts recorded two consecutive years of *significantly declining* results on provincial tests. The accountability protocol indicated that a response to such a disturbing pattern necessitated government intervention, but choosing an appropriate response involved considerable debate within the department.

In the end, it was decided to apply progressive discipline and communicate, in writing, the government's position by way of a clear statement about future consequences: "Failure to improve will result in further actions." Inserting this phrase into the letter raised anxiety levels across the region because the School Act's provision for possible actions included dismissal of the school board and nonrenewal of the superintendent's appointment. Failed leadership was no longer immune to intervention.

One year later, two of these three districts experienced a turnaround with achievement levels coding *significantly improved*. In the third district, improvement occurred but not at a statistically significant level to be coded *improved*. In 2010, all three districts achieved a coding of *significantly improved*. "Further actions" stipulated in the *letter of warning* were not required. The lesson from this is that the application of consequences to poor levels of performance improved student success in these three school districts.

Equally impressive were the results related to student achievement on the provincial report card. Provincial results for the *Acceptable Standard*—equivalent to a pass—for the three years prior to 2010 were consistently coded as *significantly declined* providing provincial leadership with considerable concern. A public report card, which was then readily available across the province, enabled the public to see the disappointing results and to apply pressure on local officials to take appropriate action.

After issuing the *warning letter* to these three districts and enduring the criticisms across the region for issuing this consequence, student achievement improved across the province. The student achievement measure recorded on the provincial report card in 2010 was coded *significantly improved*. Government's decision to *intervene* with public pressure on those responsible for the results benefited students. The whispering within borderline performance in other districts prompted increased attention affecting an uptick in provincial performance.

Pressure, through an application of negative consequences, must be a leadership consideration; however, efficacious pressure can also be created by the use of positive consequences. At the same time that the provincial government was applying progressive discipline toward the three school districts, another program was initiated to recognize and reward high levels of performance. International assessments consistently placed Alberta near the top of the global list and provincial internal test results overall were mostly at the *excellent* and *good* levels. Leadership's responsibility and commitment was to continue and improve these already high levels of performance.

Therefore, an award system for *excellent* ratings was negotiated with stakeholders. Each year, assemblies of school district officials were held when certificates listing areas of *excellent* levels of performance were recorded on the district's annual report card. Seldom were there instances when a district did not have at least one area of *excellence* that qualified for recognition, and some districts had multiple areas identified. This recognition program, focusing on school trustee and senior management, celebrated the leadership team's success and provided a model for school districts to use with *school* leadership teams in their districts.

Comparability with previous levels of performance was the mainstay; however, comparability with other district leadership teams also occurred because these celebrations included comparison with the number of categories qualifying for recognition out of approximately twenty outcomes. Incorporating recognition at the leadership level was made easier because of a corresponding program across the region which annually awarded *Teachers of Excellence*, albeit these were based on subjective criteria.

Additional disciplinary actions should be spelled out; however, eventually key leaders, including union bureaucrats, are removed from their positions. In this manner, a *shared vision* replaces the selfishness that currently exists. Trust between the partners increases because accountability for educational excellence is equalized.

Including union leadership in these accountabilities is a novel approach. Unions understand a basic accountability in the private sector where profit and loss statements prevail. These statements are lacking in the public sector where politicians merely transfer resources from one department to another or incur deficits and dig deeper into public pockets.

Increasingly, this long-standing approach to *increase spending without return on investment* is becoming politically incorrect and public attitudes are shifting. *Network*, a 1976 American satirical film selected for preservation in the United States National Film Registry by the Library of Congress is considered "culturally, historically, or aesthetically significant." The film's contribution to society is its famous line, "I'm mad as hell and I'm not going to take it anymore." Union leadership would be wise to approach the education system for a place in the tent rather than wait for political backlash from their constantly selfish pursuits.

KEY POINTS

- Students are more accountable than are their teachers.
- Many teacher evaluations are meaningless because they do not differentiate

talent or monitor degrees of success.
- While teacher evaluation expectations are increasing, the process is frequently circumvented when principals seek to avoid the discomfort of simply entering a classroom to observe teaching.
- Client (student) satisfaction surveys should be incorporated as part of the teacher evaluation process.
- Student academic growth data, as measured by standardized tests, is another controversial component in teacher evaluations.
- Teachers' cognitive skills affect student learning; however, a large percentage of American teachers graduate from the bottom portion of high school GPAs.
- Teachers receive the highest marks in university programs because of high levels of grade inflation in teacher education.
- Linking teacher pay with their student success in learning is a recent development.
- School/district and state or provincial report cards are now available to the public.
- Accountability requires consequences and team awards—including the union—are a more palatable and logical solution for recognizing superior performance.

Chapter 4

Job for Life Is a Wrong Practice

> It is true that, when an entitlement begins to be enjoyed by people, they like to keep it.
>
> —Jon Kyl

American senator Jon Kyl's words reflect a problem facing North American society where too many citizens want some form of payment or security from their government, and too many employees expect guarantees from their employers. Entitlement thinking is a curse to excellence, *and public sector employers are significant contributors in spreading the entitlement disease throughout our society.*

Job for life is one example where entitlement is straining our public sector and, specifically, education. Tenure was deemed necessary to protect teachers from capricious hiring practices in very small jurisdictions as well as for protection when teaching controversial subject matter. Today, North America is highly inhabited with a mobile worker force where replacing a teacher with an administrator's relative or friend is highly unlikely. Curriculum content, once the purview of individual schools, now is developed for entire states and provinces and poses no threat to teachers' livelihood when teaching government-approved curriculum content.

Every taxpayer should be confident that their dollars are obtaining *the highest quality* of educational services. Every parent cherishes a hope that their child will be instructed by the *best teacher*, not just once in a while but each year. Every school district should be pursuing the best teachers to put in front of their students. Every teacher should feel confident that their employer values their services, *not just in year one after being hired but every year thereafter.*

If there is any perceived ambivalence in committing toward these aspirations, the system is failing in its attempt to be student centered. It is disingenuous to make lofty claims about intent not supported by action, *but school districts routinely place less than the best teacher available in front of their students.* Even the experienced teacher may no longer demonstrate the same degree of proficiency since being hired. There are no acceptable excuses for failing to provide students with a quality education each and every year.

Many generally believe that teaching is the most important profession because it holds our future well-being: *learn well, live well.* Tenure or job for life contradicts this belief because it does not hold teachers to the highest standard of performance. One school administrator stated it well when he said, "We also want to keep pushing them, just like we want to keep pushing our kids." Yes, we value education and we expect teachers to push their students toward excellence. *Students should not experience greater accountability than the adults who serve them.* Accountability signals our respect!

Providing teachers with a job for life is really unfair to them and contributes to performance evaluations that are grossly inflated and filled with fluff. In the past, teachers were not remunerated for excellent performance, so they did not benefit from this type of reinforcement. Rather, they work in an environment where everyone is "stroked" because, when it comes time to evaluate school administrators, teacher perceptions frequently are included as a significant measure. Education suffers too much from *mutual backslapping.*

TEACHER EVALUATIONS DEMONSTRATE LOW STANDARDS

Raising this significant issue is not intended to denigrate the teaching profession: merely a desire to recognize people in a legitimate fashion for their performance. Very likely, more evaluations are written on teachers than any other profession. Unfortunately, the evidence is that these evaluations are mainly perfunctory and meaningless. Virtually every teacher passes the test of *minimal competence* in a profession characterized by low standards, and almost all teachers are rated *above average,* which is obviously impossible.

A U.S. study conducted by *Public Agenda* in 2003 polled 1,345 schoolteachers on a variety of educational issues, including the role that tenure played in their schools. When asked, "Does tenure mean that a teacher has worked hard and proved themselves to be very good at what they do?" a response by 58 percent of the teachers polled answered that no, tenure "does not necessarily" mean that. In a related question, 78 percent said a few (or more) teachers in their schools "fail to do a good job and are simply going through the motions." *Teachers understand that tenure is not equated with excellence.* In fact, it is not even indicative of satisfactory performance.

The McGrath Training Systems website (https://www.mcgrathtraining.com/) summarizes why they perceive tenure to be an "awful" characteristic in the education system:

> For more than 20 years, we have been gathering the responses of 150,000-plus school site administrators to our anecdotal survey regarding the performance of school district teachers, and their evaluations. We have found that between three percent and five percent of permanent teachers are functioning in the lowest category of "poor." Another thirteen percent to twenty percent need improvement to meet satisfactory performance and can be considered marginal. However, school site administrators admit that in their districts, the number of teachers who receive an unsatisfactory performance rating can be counted on one hand, with several fingers spared. So, an average of twenty-five percent of teachers nationwide has some need for performance improvement, but do not receive an evaluation that reflects that. Therefore, no improvement occurs. That is the scandal. (N.p.)

McGrath's research demonstrates that having a tenured teacher in front of a class is no guarantee that students receive quality instructional services. However, tenure is a bedrock issue with unions. While holding tenaciously to this practice absolutely refutes that they are student centered, they know that they hold the upper hand in protecting their members. *Excellence is not their mantra; protection is.* Their ability to control management is a higher priority than the well-being of the nation. They want the public to believe that teaching is the most important profession, but their actions demonstrate a different perspective.

Some educators undoubtedly chafe at the suggestion that teachers, in most instances, receive a job for life. Occasionally these objections are legitimate;

however, new teachers in most regions receive a permanent contract that is for life unless layoffs are necessary. These staff reductions are the result of extenuating circumstances which happen occasionally and cannot be avoided. The irony is that the longer a teacher is employed and possesses many years of seniority, the more unlikely they will experience even the threat of a layoff.

Proponents of tenure argue that tenure protects teachers from being replaced by less expensive and, presumably, less-skilled new teachers. *This argument is indicative of the fallacy surrounding the myth that experience is the determinant of excellence.* If such was the case, why would employers want to replace an older *superstar* with a younger inferior teacher? The answer is simple! Until recently, education did not formally recognize that some teachers are superior to others, and we did not utilize measures of superior performance in holding educators accountable, or *even in celebrating their talent.*

Debating tenure necessitates responding to a central question not particularly understood in public debate. *Are teachers interchangeable*? Putting aside differences in specialization such as having a social studies teach mathematics, are accredited teachers equally competent? Parents understand that there are differences in teacher competence but is this awareness fully understood? Gorman (2005), summarizing the work of Hanushek et al. (2005), quantifies teachers' impact on student achievement:

> Good teachers increase student achievement. The average student who has a good teacher at the 85th quality percentile can expect annual achievement gains that are 0.22 standard deviations greater than the average student with a median teacher. Good teachers do well with students at all levels of achievement, and there is no evidence that teacher education . . . contributes to quality teaching. (n.p.)

This conclusion compares teachers viewed as good compared with medium. What about those *below* medium and how much impact on student success occurs when there is such variance in performance? Hanushek's conclusion is that the estimated difference in annual achievement growth between having a good and having a bad teacher can be *more than one grade-level equivalent in test performance.* This large discrepancy in student success should be a concern for any parent but can be even more alarming when the experience is repeated.

Too frequently, the "dance of the lemons," which describes how *poor teachers* are frequently moved from one school to another, places them in schools serving low socioeconomic students. Their parents appear to be less likely to complain about the quality of their child's teacher. One superintendent observed how, when his district went through the annual year-end transfer of teachers, problem teachers tended to be placed in the district's poorer areas in his community.

Dillon (2011) reported on Michelle Rhee's reform efforts in teacher evaluation in the District of Columbia noting that 35 percent of the teachers in the city's wealthiest area were rated "highly effective" compared with only 5 percent in the poorest. The chances are disturbingly high that students in the lower socioeconomic regions will experience several years with mediocre teachers. In effect, a risk for these students living in these poorer areas is that increased exposure to mediocrity exacerbates their likelihood of lower levels of achievement and increased likelihood of remaining poor.

The mistake made by the public is their belief that "as long as there is an accredited teacher—any teacher—in front of the classroom, students are being served adequately" (Weisberg et al. 2009). The assumption that teachers are interchangeable is reprehensible because,

> School systems wrongly conflate educational access with educational quality; the only teacher quality that schools need to achieve is to fill all of their positions. . . . Give high need students three highly effective teachers in a row and they may outperform students taught by three ineffective teachers in a row by as much as 50 percentile points. (p.9)

In Washington, D.C., Lewin (2010) posted that School Chancellor Rhee's reform for dealing with underperforming teachers culminated with the dismissal of almost 1,000 teachers during her three-year tenure. Between the years 2007–2013, The *Washington Post* (https://www.washingtonpost.com/news/answer-sheet/wp/2014/08/05/if-this-isnt-school-reform-failure-what-is/) released student achievement test results for D.C. showing scores of *Proficient* or *Advanced* improving from 27 percent to 50 percent in mathematics and from 34 percent to 47 percent in reading. Dismissing more than one-quarter of the district's teachers produced phenomenally improved levels of student achievement.

Jensen and Reichl (2011) provide additional perspectives regarding teacher's potential for making significant contributions to student achievement,

> Conservative estimates suggest that a student with a teacher at the 75th percentile of effectiveness (measured with a value-added metric) will achieve in three-quarters of a year what a student with a teacher at the 25th percentile will achieve in a full year. A student with an excellent teacher (at the 90th percentile) would achieve in *half a year* what a student with a less effective teacher (at the 10th percentile) will learn in *a full year*. (p.6)

Barber and Mourshed (2007) summarize the large differences they discovered when comparing student success during instruction from high- and low-performing teachers:

- High-performing teachers have students progress three times as fast as when with low-performing teachers.
- In primary grades, students placed with consecutive low-performing teachers suffer educational loss which is *irreversible*.
- A teacher's level of literacy, as measured by standardized tests, affects student achievement more than any other measurable teacher attribute.

It is safe to say that these gains or losses, as the case may be, are cumulative when students benefit or are disadvantaged with a preponderance of higher or lower level performing teachers.

This discussion about the large differences in success experienced within teacher ranks is really about *employers abrogating their socially mandated right and responsibility to manage the resources in our educational systems in a way that benefits children.* There are many occasions during contract negotiations when the employer demonstrates whether or not the outcome will be *student or employee centered.* Providing teachers with a job for life is an example of an irresponsible give away that neither serves the client nor reflects good management.

Schools perpetually look for improvement strategies which, unfortunately, usually increase expenditures in frivolous and unjustified ways, just as politicians are prone to do in other spheres of public finance. Rather than tackle reforms that will improve quality and achieve better services at a lower cost, administrators shy away from tackling *entrenched* and sensitive systemic issues, such as tenure, preferring instead to appeal to opportunistic politicians to provide increased funding. Whenever they do this, they contribute to the rapidly rising cost of education and *create benefit for special interest groups rather than students.*

THE SUCCESS OF TEACHERS' UNIONS

Teacher unions are complicit in this matter because they are more focused on their mandate to protect their members, especially the weaker ones, than they are on providing students with quality education. It is not an exaggeration to say that unions have been extremely successful in providing their members with a job for life.

Using a *whipsaw strategy* that played one employer off against others and then claiming, "if there, why not here," unions gradually handicapped the educational system. For this reason, it is not possible to believe their claims of having the students' best interests in mind and their protestations that they know best what is needed to improve the system.

Unions represent a powerful political force that takes advantage of an *uninformed* public who do not understand the stark difference in objectives between the well-intentioned teacher in their school and the quenchless thirst for power exhibited by union leaders. Their position of power is enhanced when their thirst is accompanied by the *right to strike*, which inconveniences parents who require custodial care for their children.

When parents and their children are *held hostage by a withdrawal of educational services*, they have little understanding of the complex issues the employer is attempting to ameliorate. Their impatience is frequently verbalized by comments such as "just get this settled!" Parents' desperate need for children's custodial care during a strike is the union's trump card in achieving their outcomes.

Providing teachers with a job for life suggests that teachers are essentially infallible. The implication is that their *intrinsic motivation to excel is high every day, every month, and every year for several decades.* In addition to this, it holds that the teacher will immediately pursue improvement in the workplace as education changes. It also assumes that curriculum changes will be implemented vigorously even when a teacher is within five years of retirement. In reality, however, their personal perspectives and circumstances, which made them such desirable employees at hiring, may not remain so for decades without additional pressure being applied to their motivation.

Above all, the job-for-life situation in education is a condition that says all other professions have it wrong. At least, careers outside of the public sector have it wrong, because the private sector has accountabilities that provide a check and balance throughout a career. If clients do not value someone's services, they will not engage in a contract to employ that company or individual, whether it is to fix their car, toilet, eyes, or build their house.

People working in sales understand how quickly accountability impacts their work. Many work in jobs where commissions are the only income: if nothing is sold nothing is earned. There also are examples within the sales sector of companies releasing the bottom producer at the end of each month. The virtual job-for-life environment in education is in stark contrast to the accountabilities in the private sector and is a working condition of incalculable worth; yet, once identified as the reason for lower salaries in the public sector.

The adequacy of a job-for-life approach within education could be tested by principals if they put a sign-up list on the school door for their child's next year's teachers. Variances in the number of clients signing up for teachers would make the principal's task unbearable. The most latitude available to parents in this regard is for the principal to let parents know that a request can be initiated, but with no guarantee that it will be accommodated.

From experience, many parents are leery about ramifications that they might be attempting to avoid specific teachers and will not initiate a request, and the principal is able to accommodate requests from those who have. Unfettered choice accommodated by posting sign-up sheets would create administrative havoc such as principals forcing students into specific classrooms.

Job tenure for teachers has destabilized the working relationship with the employer and shifted the balance of power to the employed. A superintendent explained the consequences of this imbalance when he repeated his school-trustees' instructions. They saw every hiring decision as a thirty-five-year commitment. Therefore, he was literally ordered to meet personally with every potential new hiring before contracts were signed so that he would become accountable for the selection. Whenever a problem occurred with a teacher, board members immediately queried whether this superintendent had vetted the selection personally.

In order to protect himself, this superintendent began to contact various agencies and organizations in an effort to discover the most powerful "listen-for" in the candidate's responses. Recruiters were trained in this technique, and went through the same process hundreds of times annually to ferret out teachers who could verbalize how they implemented desirable teaching characteristics.

Whatever methods school districts use to identify talented teachers, there are no guarantees that the new hires will possess the same talent a few years later. A principal demonstrated a systemic weakness in education when he responded to a question of why his school was selected as the top school in America. It was not an advantaged school serving a high socioeconomic community. Rather it was situated along the U.S./Mexico border in San Diego with a diversified student population. Walking through the school and interacting with students revealed how special this school was and why news media networks were descending upon this community.

The principal's response to why the school was so successful was worthy of the secrecy he used in providing it. Rather than blurt out a comment for all those assembled, he convened a one-on-one meeting in the privacy of his office where he had a better chance of controlling the consequences of verbalizing his confidential response. The bottom line, in his opinion, was that every teacher on staff was working on *a one-year contract*. Theirs was not a job for life! Indeed, if the contract was not renewed, they were released from the school district as well.

This charter school produced performance at a high standard resulting in public adulation. Children *were* the first priority. This gave his school an unfair advantage because other schools were unable to achieve similarly high levels of service. Was being fair to their students unfair and wrong? Should this community be penalized by having their school downgraded to the level of schooling provided across the region or the nation? Should other schools not benefiting from this provision receive an apology from the school district's administration for not being able to provide a similar service to their children?

The answer to these questions is obvious. When we know a best practice, it should be made available to every learning environment. It is justified to borrow the union's battle cry: "if there, why not here?" Politicians should have the courage to respond accordingly, but they hesitate because it will cost them votes in their next election and funding for their campaigns. Most compromise their principles by choosing the politically correct path and favoring special interests and not their students.

Whatever the well-meaning intentions were initially, today the main function of tenure is to subjugate students' rights and help poor teachers keep their jobs. Former D.C. schools chancellor Michelle Rhee (https://www.debate.org/debates/There-should-not-be-a-teacher-tenure./1/) bluntly portrayed tenure as "the holy grail of teacher unions, but it has no educational value for kids; it only benefits adults" (n.p.).

Once a teacher is assured of tenure, his or her motivation to excel is lost. Teachers today not only decide how and when there will be a change in practice or in the implementation of the curriculum, but they also decide whether such change will even take place. Providing high levels of service to students is less likely because employment uncertainties are almost nonexistent. As long as the teacher is assessed as being *minimally* competent, he or she survives.

It may be that for many the idea that teachers in the public system would work under the same conditions as those employed in charter schools is too radical. This would mean contracts could be for as short a period as ten months. However, *it does not seem unreasonable to ask that contracts be set at three to five years, and not for life.* Teachers who continue to practice their craft proficiently could qualify for contract renewals within their *district knowing that they are perceived as valuable when a new contract is issued.* A sense of fulfillment is more likely to occur when there are more frequent opportunities to express appreciation for a level of service.

Another approach is to establish a teacher evaluation system that *employs multiple ratings.* Many systems only utilize a pass or fail conclusion. In a multiple rating system, teachers with the higher ratings might qualify for a two- or three-year contract for "satisfactory" performance but receive accreditation involving a longer term—for example, five years—for "outstanding" performance. This type of system acknowledges that no one is immune from societal factors which result in lower levels of performance in their work.

THE TENURE TIDE IS CHANGING

Proponents of tenure may argue that employers have ample opportunity to assess teaching talent while the teacher is on probation: usually the first one or two years of their employment. But is it realistic to assume strong performance will follow for more than three decades? Garrett (quoted in UKEssays, "Should Teachers Get Tenure?" n.p.) reporting on a University of Washington study related to reinventing public education found that the first two to three years of teaching do not predict post-tenure performance. Our workplace in a global village is complex and it is not surprising that our workforce must be flexible in meeting changing needs.

Motivation to change practices frequently emerges from data demonstrating intolerable situations. Weisberg et al. (2009) with the New Teacher Project found that 81 percent of school administrators knew a poorly performing tenured teacher at their school. This study indicated that the untenable revelation is the result of 86 percent of administrators indicating that they did not pursue dismissal of teachers because of the costly and time-consuming process. McGuinn (2010), for example, reported that it can take up to 335 days to remove a tenured teacher before the courts get involved.

A few American politicians have *rattled this cage* to remove tenure. On July 24, 2009, then U.S. President Barack Obama and Secretary of Education Arne Duncan announced the *Race to the Top* program. This initiative made available $4.35 billion in grants to encourage and reward states that are creating the conditions for education innovation and reform. Requirements for states to receive funding from the new federal program included adopting policies that take into account student achievement when evaluating teachers, and having plans to remove ineffective tenured and untenured teachers.

This pronouncement precipitated attitudinal shifts in places such as New York City, where Baker (2012) summarized the changing landscape in *The New York Times:*

> Nearly half of New York City teachers reaching the end of their probations were denied tenure this year, the Education Department said on Friday, marking the culmination of years of efforts toward Mayor Michael R. Bloomberg's goal to end "tenure as we know it." Only 55 percent of eligible teachers, having worked for at least three years, earned tenure in 2012, compared with 97 percent in 2007. An additional 42 percent this year were kept on probation for another year, and 3 percent were denied tenure and fired. Of those whose probations were extended last year, fewer than half won tenure this year, a third was given yet another year to prove themselves, and 16 percent were denied tenure or resigned. (N.p.)

An apple is frequently used as a symbol for education, and an idiom describing this trending away from tenure is that the *bite into the apple has revealed a worm.* In other words, something viewed from the outside and as a good thing has turned out to be bad. More lawmakers are demonstrating courage to tighten the requirements for earning and keeping tenure. Idaho removed tenure entirely, and Florida requires all newly hired teachers to earn an *annual* contract. New Jersey also overhauled its tenure laws making it easier to fire teachers for poor performance.

These states will be watched by others who may then determine whether they, too, will gain more support than is lost. This is the nature of politics that cannot be underestimated. It is impractical, and perhaps too counterintuitive, to think that politicians will respond automatically in doing something that is in the best interests of students merely because it is in the longer-term best interests of the state or nation. Political decisions, it seems, have to be put onto the balance scale to determine where the assets are greatest.

Perhaps politicians will receive sufficient motivation to discontinue the practice of providing tenure when the conclusions of the Howell et al. (2011) survey of 2,600 Americans are widely circulated; it revealed from the opinionated responses that 49 percent opposed teacher tenure while 20 percent supported it. Despite this weak public support for tenure, the reality that politicians face is that tenure is the *Holy Grail* for teachers which, by itself, can determine where a teacher will place an "X" when they are in the voting booth. Everyone supports accountability until it is in my own place of work.

On the other hand, few members of the general public are similarly focused on this issue when they decide where the "X" should go. A politician's election promise to remove teacher tenure may not be their determining factor in where to place the "X" on the ballot. On the other hand, teachers comprise a large work group within the workforce and politicians have to weigh the consequences of alienating them on an issue that will galvanize their opposition.

If the political route is too difficult, there may be a glimmer of hope on another horizon if what Knowles (2010) writes is generalizable across school districts regarding a survey of teachers in the American Federation of Teachers.

> The good news is that the majority of teachers are not interested in protecting colleagues who don't belong in the classroom. Last summer the American Federation of Teachers surveyed its members, asking: "Which of these should

be the higher priority: working for professional teaching standards and good teaching, or defending the job rights of teachers who face disciplinary action?" According to Randi Weingarten, the union's president, "by a ratio of 4 to 1 (69% to 16%), AFT members chose working for professional standards and good teaching as the higher priority." She elaborated: "Teachers have zero tolerance for people who . . . demonstrate they are unfit for our profession." (N.p.)

Knowles indicates that in the United States, between 0.1 percent and 1 percent of tenured teachers are dismissed annually, according to the Center for American Progress. His conclusion is that,

> The time has come to eliminate tenure. We are facing monumental challenges in our quest to provide all students with an education that will prepare them to compete in a globalized economy. By removing one of the main sources of friction between labor and management, we can focus on the substantive issues: training, evaluating and rewarding teachers to make teaching a true profession. (N.p.)

According to Knowles, tenure is one of the main sources of friction between labor and management.

The bottom line in this debate about tenure for teachers is that good practitioners will always be sought by employers. *It is the weak ones who are protected by tenure provisions.* Is this the right focus? Is this practice providing the best service to our nation's children? The union's *Holy Grail* is finally being challenged, and momentum to serve students' interests more than staff's self-interests will increase.

Having a formal celebration event occur routinely every few years, where the employer's representatives confirm that they want the employment relationship to continue is a more meaningful affirmation of someone's contribution. An employer's commitment to renew the relationship is the highest form of praise next to those relationships based entirely on commission, where value is communicated almost instantaneously.

KEY POINTS

- Tenure protects mediocrity and can prevent students benefiting from the best teachers.

- Accountability signals our level of respect for services.
- Teachers understand that tenure is not equated with excellence.
- The estimated difference in annual achievement growth between having a good and having a bad teacher can be more than one grade level equivalent in test performance.
- Unions are more interested in serving the needs of teacher members than student clients.
- One-year contracts are an effective alternative to job-for-life arrangements or, at the minimum, should be renewable every five years.
- Teachers' performance contracts should utilize multiple ratings of performance.

Chapter 5

Standardized Tests Are an Unwelcome Messenger

Some skeptics discount the relative-age-effect outlined in chapter 2 because much of the data utilized in these analyses is based on standardized test results. Some education stakeholders endeavor to persuade the public, including parents, that standardized tests are inaccurate measures of student achievement and should be avoided. This opposition is usually the result of increased accountability placed on educators where consequences, including pay for performance, are applied. This chapter proves the oppositional voices are false!

These voices fail to recognize that teachers constantly make use of standardized tests in their classrooms *because the working definition of a standardized test is any test given to two or more people.* Classroom teachers constantly utilize spelling tests, quizzes, end of chapter and unit tests, commercially prepared tests as well as tests they prepare on their own. To vilify system wide, standardized tests are really a smokescreen to avoid efforts at accountability for student achievement.

Some educators express their opposition to the administration of these tests because they are used with more than one class, school or school district in order for student achievement to be assessed across a school, district, or region. *In other words, it is the ability to provide comparative data concerning student achievement that creates anxieties for people in the education system who feel insecure.*

Yet, this type of information is what the public wants and needs to know. Parents want to know which teachers in their child's school have a talent for adding value to student achievement. Every educator impacts student achievement! The significant question is whether that impact is positive or negative? When standardized tests are given in many classrooms throughout a region, the answer to this question can be ascertained and the impact measured.

In an effort to address the concerns of reticent teachers and administrators, our region instituted a "balanced approach" to accountability. This meant that monitoring grade-level achievement for grades 1–9 provided an *assessment by the classroom teacher*. The blend of objective classroom assessment with teacher observation, which was based in theory on all aspects of the curriculum, was laudable, but this approach to assessment includes moving standards that are idiosyncratic to each teacher. This makes comparison between individuals and groups problematic.

This is not simply because teachers are inconsistent in the way they apply standards, although this is a significant challenge in and of itself. The other problem arises from the fact that teachers bring varying philosophies into the assessment matrix. During a presentation in Atlanta, where there were about 2000 educators in attendance, Robert Marzano presented ten marks for a course's assessment and then asked the educator audience to provide the final mark.

With everyone looking at the same information and applying their own perspectives, final marks ranged from "A" to "F" or 90 percent to 30 percent. Such a lack of consistency is customary because teachers, consciously or unconsciously, draw on their grading policy when they mark an assignment and compile results for a cumulative grade. The inconsistency occurs because educational systems too frequently delegate assessment policies to individual teachers.

For example, a teacher must decide on how incomplete assignments should be scored, what to do with assignments that are submitted, and how to respond to suspected cheating. There is also the issue of weighted scores: should they give a greater value to tests at the end of the course, and how does one assess the relative value of daily assignments or written homework and in class tests.

Then there are issues of neatness, precision, accuracy in spelling, stylistic features, and grammar—all of which are likely to vary from assignment to assignment and certainly from teacher to teacher. These and similar questions are usually handled by individual teachers and involve some philosophical grounding.

GRADE INFLATION IN THE UNITED STATES

American studies reveal extensive grade inflation across their high schools. A study (https://twitter.com/AICUOhio/status/897865658624618496) from UCLA, for example, examined applicants' high school marks every ten years and reported substantial increases in "A" letter grades. For example, 1966 grads reported 11.3 percent "A" grades, 1996 grads reported 31.5 percent, and 2016 reported 55.1 percent "A" letter grades.

Further, https://www.gradeinflation.com/ reveals how an "A" is now the most popular mark across America. Using five-year increments, the grade point average for all schools in 1983 was approximately 2.83, but by 2013 rose to almost 3.2. *Higher marks make parents, students, and the general public believe that the school system is improving.*

Grade Inflation Is Not Uniformly Evident

Grade inflation, because of low standards in our classrooms, is a documented problem virtually universal across North America. *Numbers don't lie* and the concern should be more than disconcerting: *it should be distressing.* There is no value to our society by giving *undeserved* credit to students or by *defrauding* taxpayers, the clients of our school system, of the full value of their tax dollars. The greatest harm is perpetuated in our workforce that *is developing a mindset that maximum effort is not necessary.*

Inconsistent classroom assessment of students' academic achievement is a long-standing problem that is too frequently disregarded because the information is not transparently presented for public scrutiny. While this lack of transparency is an issue, *inflated marks are seldom disputed by students or their parents,* especially when the pattern shows that these high marks are not irregular blips but an ongoing problem throughout the school system.

This evidence about low standards in classrooms demonstrates how inconsistent teachers are when assessing their students' achievement. Our focus is answering the question about whether grade inflation is uniformly evident across students, *because unfairness applied equally to everyone can still be considered fair. Unfairness rears its head when consistency is lacking.* Is there, then, another inconsistency that must be monitored by administrators seeking to ensure fairness to students? Specifically, does grade inflation occur equally across all student populations?

Grade Inflation and Gender Unfairness in British Columbia

A suitable means for answering this question concerning fairness is a comment made by British Columbia's Education Department when they responded to our request for information. Specifically, "Provincial reports indicate a relatively high correlation between the classroom and exam marks across gender and do not suggest that classroom marks exhibit gender unfairness." An analysis of their 2015 school year results makes it difficult to corroborate their conclusion. This jurisdiction masks the degree to which the problem exists by rolling up the higher-achieving marks with C+, B, and A into one category.

- **English 10**: The advantage (scoring C+, B, or A) accorded to female students on the *exam* is 13 percent but in *classrooms* is 18 percent or *plus 5 percent*.
- **Math 10 (Pre Calc):** The advantage (scoring C+, B, or A) accorded to female students on the exam is 1 percent but in classrooms is 6 percent or *plus 5 percent*.
- **Math 10 (App):** The advantage (scoring C+, B, or A) accorded to female students on the exam is *minus* 6 percent but in classrooms is plus 3 percent or *plus 9 percent*.
- **Science 10:** The advantage (scoring C+, B, or A) accorded to female students on the exam is 1 percent but in classrooms is 9 percent or *plus 8 percent*.
- **Social Studies 11**: The advantage (scoring C+, B, or A) accorded to female students on the exam is *minus* 1 percent but in classrooms is 13 percent or *plus 14 percent*.
- **Civic Studies 11**: The advantage (scoring C+, B, or A) accorded to female students on the exam is *minus* 1 percent but in classrooms is plus 18 percent or *plus 19 percent*.
- **BC First Nations Studies**: The advantage (scoring C+, B, or A) accorded to female students on the exam is 10 percent but in classrooms is 23 percent

or *plus 13 percent*.
- **English 12:** The advantage (scoring C+, B, or A) accorded to female students on the exam is 8 percent and in classrooms is 12 percent, or *plus 4 percent*.
- **English 12 First Peoples:** The advantage (scoring C+, B, or A) accorded to female students on the exam is 18 percent and in classrooms is 24 percent, *or plus 6 percent*.
- **Communications 12:** The advantage (scoring C+, B, or A) accorded to female students on the exam is 3 percent and in classrooms is 14 percent, *or plus 11 percent*.

In each subject, female students were given C+, B, or A class marks more frequently than their male counterparts, which is not the issue. Rather, comparing these class marks with the provincial examination marks reveals our concern that the female advantage, when comparing the differences between class marks and provincial examination marks, teacher-generated marks *always favor females* by a considerably larger percentage. We can conclude that some teacher bias occurs which places males at a disadvantage whenever these assessments are used for awards, scholarships, and placement in university programs.

Gender Unfairness in Alberta

Alberta's student enrollment corresponds to a mid-sized American state. Grade twelve students write provincial school-leaving exit tests—Diploma Examinations—after January and June semesters. Marks on these examinations are combined with class marks from teachers for a final mark on the students' transcripts. An analysis for the *Standard of Excellence* and *Acceptable Standard* of 2016 marks based on gender follows and records how many more female students than males achieved each standard. (*A negative sign depicts males having a higher percentage.*)

These *January results* (table 5.1) demonstrate how females were awarded more *Standard of Excellence* marks from their teachers in *every subject*; however, females outscored the males only in five tests on the standardized provincial examinations marked *anonymously by a team of teachers in the provincial marking center*. The prevalence of high marks from classroom teachers provided females an advantage in nine of the ten courses, and this

Table 5.1 January 2016: Standard of Excellence (Equivalent to an "A"). (Example: In ELA 30-2, 67 percent more females received *Excellence* from their teacher. In the provincial exam, 26 percent more females received *Excellence*. The female advantage from their teachers' mark is 41 percent.)

Subject	School Mark (%)	Diploma Exam (%)	Female Advantage (%)
ELA 30-2	67	26	41
ELA 30-1	48	53	−5
Math 30-1	8	−5	13
Math 30-2	59	50	9
Biology	5	−4	9
Science	31	27	4
Chemistry	2	−7	9
Physics	13	1	12
Social Studies 30-1	19	−14	33
Social Studies 30-2	33	−1	34

advantage provides more opportunity for *awards, scholarships, and placement in university programs*. The overall advantage for females from high-class marks is 15.9 percent.

These *June results* (table 5.2) demonstrate how females were awarded more *Standard of Excellence* marks from their teachers in every subject except Chemistry which was equal; however, females outscored the males only in five tests on the standardized provincial examinations marked *anonymously*. The prevalence of high marks from classroom teachers provided females an advantage in nine of the ten courses, and this advantage provides more *opportunity for awards, scholarships, and placement in university programs*. The overall advantage for females from high-class marks is 18.5 percent.

Combining the January and June test administrations reveals that female students were awarded more *Standard of Excellence* in nineteen of the twenty *classroom assessments*: June's Chemistry was the exception with 0 percent. However, using the system's diploma examinations, females and males had an equal number of test administrations with the higher percentage scoring *Standard of Excellence*. Examining the upper stream courses important for university applications, males outscored females at the *Standard of Excellence* on eight of the twelve administrations.

These January results (table 5.3) demonstrate how females were *failed* less frequently by their teachers in every subject; however, females were failed

Table 5.2 June 2016: Standard of Excellence (Equivalent to an "A").

Subject	School Mark (%)	Diploma Exam (%)	Female Advantage (%)
ELA 30-2	63	29	34
ELA 30-1	39	20	19
Math 30-1	6	−2	8
Math 30-2	40	56	−16
Biology	3	−7	10
Science	39	9	30
Chemistry	0	−15	15
Physics	15	0	15
Social Studies 30-1	15	−3	18
Social Studies 30-2	35	−1	36

Table 5.3 January 2016: Not Achieving the Acceptable Standard. (Did *not* meet and therefore must retake the course.) (Example: In ELA 30-2, 95 percent *more males* were assessed as "failed" from their teacher. In the provincial exam, 13 percent more males failed. The female advantage from the school mark is 82 percent fewer failed or almost double.)

Subject	School Mark (%)	Diploma Exam (%)	Female Advantage (%)
ELA 30-2	−95	−13	82
ELA 30-1	−110	−8	102
Math 30-1	−42	−1	41
Math 30-2	−67	−36	31
Biology	−9	4	13
Science	−92	−2	90
Chemistry	−12	−2	10
Physics	−128	−13	115
Social Studies 30-1	−17	27	44
Social Studies 30-2	−42	17	59

at a higher percentage on three of the standardized provincial examinations marked anonymously. Viewing class marks and provincial tests together, the third column demonstrates how much females are advantaged by having such large discrepancies between the two types of assessments.

These June results (table 5.4) demonstrate how females were failed less frequently by their teachers in every subject; however, females were failed at a higher percentage on five of the *standardized provincial examinations marked anonymously*. Viewing class marks and provincial tests together,

Table 5.4 June 2016: Not Achieving the Acceptable Standard. (Did *not* meet and therefore must retake the course.) (Example: In ELA 30-2, 36 percent more males were assessed as "failed" from their teacher. In the provincial exam, 12 percent more males failed. The female advantage from the school mark is 24 percent fewer failed.)

Subject	School Mark (%)	Diploma Exam (%)	Female Advantage (%)
ELA 30-2	−36	−12	24
ELA 30-1	−43	−4	39
Math 30-1	−48	2	50
Math 30-2	−55	−30	25
Biology	−6	3	9
Science	−62	−1	61
Chemistry	−20	12	32
Physics	−124	−6	118
Social Studies 30-1	−30	31	−1
Social Studies 30-2	−57	11	68

the third column demonstrates how much females are advantaged by having such large discrepancies between the two types of assessments. High levels of grade inflation evident within class assessments by teachers, *who are not marking students anonymously*, compensate females' lower achievement on provincial standardized tests.

Notably, on Social Studies 30-1, females were failed in their class marks less frequently than males by 30 percent; however, on the provincial diploma examination, females failed 31 percent more frequently which placed them at an overall disadvantage by 1 percent. In Physics, females' classroom failure rates were 124 percent fewer than the rate for males; yet, they failed the diploma examination more frequently (6 percent) but still were advantaged by 118 percent fewer failures when combining the two sets of marks.

It is also noteworthy that on the twenty examinations during these two semesters, only on two occasions—that is, ELA 30-1 @ −5 percent and Math 30-2 @ −16 percent—were females disadvantaged when comparing *Standard of Excellence* class marks with the provincial examination marks. Females were disadvantaged only in one subject (Social Studies 30-1 @-1 percent) when conducting a similar comparison combining marks for meeting the *Acceptable Standard*.

In the run-up to the provincial election in 2015, the government sought to pander for the teachers' union support by altering the weighting of the two components leading to students' final mark. The standard through many decades was to weight the class marks equally (50/50) with the provincial diploma exam. Beginning in 2016, government *implemented a new weighting with class marks accounting for 70 percent making this component more than twice the value of the provincial tests which were professionally prepared, extensively field tested, and marked anonymously.*

Table 5.5 provides an example of how the new formula (70/30) exaggerates further the advantage females enjoyed in table 6.1 (January 2016: *Standard of Excellence* (Equivalent to an "A").

The revised blended grading instituted by government is misleading, particularly when the school-awarded mark and diploma examination mark diverge. A confidential email from the provincial examination manager revealed a situation with a school where there was a:

Class averaging over 80% on the school-awarded mark and less than 50% on the Diploma Examination mark. The resulting blended average; a grade likely in the low 70% range (under the new 70/30 blend) *is not the result of any assessment evidence justifying this grade,* yet this grade could be used to determine a student's post-secondary eligibility.

Grade inflation occurring in classrooms further inflated by a factor of 2.3 in the 70/30 newly adopted *weighting regime clearly identifies which gender will win future awards, scholarships, and placements in university programs.*

Table 5.5 January 2016: Standard of Excellence (Equivalent to an "A") with Impact of 70/30 Weighting in Favor of Class Mark Indicated in Brackets and Italics.

Subject	School Mark	Diploma Exam	Female Advantage
ELA 30-2	67% *(154%)*	26%	41% *(128%)*
ELA 30-1	48% (110%)	53%	−5% *(57%)*
Math 30-1	8% *(23%)*	−5%	13% *(23%)*
Math 30-2	59% *(136%)*	50%	9% *(86%)*
Biology	5% *(12%)*	−4%	9% *(16%)*
Science	31% *(71%)*	27%	4% *(44%)*
Chemistry	2% *(5%)*	−7%	9% *(12%)*
Physics	13% *(30%)*	1%	12% *(31%)*
Social Studies 30-1	19% *(44%)*	−14%	33% *(58%)*
Social Studies 30-2	33% *(76%)*	−1%	34% *(75%)*

For example, Alberta has two major universities—Edmonton and Calgary—and their undergraduate enrollment already reports a decided advantage for female students. In U of A (Edmonton), for example, there were 12,962 males and 16,138 females registered in their public report (2011) providing females with 55.5 percent of placements. In Calgary, their 2015 report provided placements for 10,667 males and 12,146 females resulting in 53.3 percent placements for female students. *The female ratio will increase substantially with the government's decision to weight class marks higher by a factor of 2.3:1.*

Grade Inflation's Gender Advantage

The foregoing provides evidence of the female gender advantage in British Columbia and Alberta, two high achieving school systems on the *PISA 2018 assessments of fifteen-year-old* students. The problem of grade inflation continually begs the question regarding whether every student has an inflated mark or only some students? Unfairness occurs when different criteria are used when students' work is assessed.

Douglas Reeves, an American expert on assessment, provided an insightful exchange of e-mails when he stated, "Teacher bias that I have observed is most insidious not in the tests themselves, but in the conflation of academic performance and behavior when translating test performance into marks for the report card." If behavior influences student letter grades, are there some whose behavior advantages them more than others?

If there is a discernible pattern that demonstrates a bias, then the issue of fairness rears its ugly head. Reeves explains,

> Students (disproportionately minority girls in my research) receive higher letter grades for lower actual achievement, because of their quiet, compliant and respectful attitude. I will note, parenthetically, that I'm all in favor of quiet, compliant and respectful behavior among teenagers—I just wish that we would not call these characteristics "algebra" or "physics."

Webber et al. (2009) similarly concluded that culture influenced student marks in their conclusion that almost 60 percent of educators perceived that students' cultural background affected the grades these students got.

Reeves explains further how the bias serves to *disadvantage male students*, and adds the observation that teachers readily discern a dichotomy between test and class marks:

Other students (disproportionately boys) receive lower letter grades for higher actual achievement, because of disorganization and oppositional behavior. Every time I ask teachers if they can think of students who make A's and B's on tests yet receive D's or F's in the class, almost every hand goes up.

Harlen (2004), synthesizing *twenty-three studies* from the United Kingdom and United States, also concluded that evidence of gender bias exists by stating, "Teachers' judgments of the academic performance of young children are influenced by the teachers' assessment of their behavior; this adversely affects the assessment of boys compared with girls" (n.p.). Scantelbury (2009) stated it somewhat differently by saying, "Overall, teachers have lower expectations for girls' academic success compared to boys" (n.p.).

Webber et al. (2009), after surveying and interviewing teachers, found that a surprisingly high percentage of teachers acknowledged a *gender bias*. Almost 1 in 4 (23 percent) of educators agreed "students' gender" affected the grades they get. However, their qualitative data suggested that gender was frequently linked with behavior in that boys were perceived to be more disruptive and less compliant, which, in turn, influenced the grades that teachers assigned to boys. Levels of compliance affected course grading.

Gender bias toward female students has also attracted the attention of the OECD's PISA tests involving more than sixty countries. Coughlan (2015) reported that

> teachers are more lenient in their marking of girls' schoolwork, according to an international study. An OECD report on gender in education, across more than 60 countries, found that girls receive higher marks compared with boys of the same ability. Researchers suggest girls are better behaved in class and this influences how teachers perceive their work.
>
> Differences in school results can sometimes "have little to do with ability," says the study.
>
> The OECD study, examining gender inequality in education . . . reveals that teachers can be biased towards giving girls higher results than boys, even when they have produced the same quality of work. The researchers suggest that this reflects expectations about girls being positive towards learning and less disruptive.

> When it comes to teachers' marking, the study says there is a consistent pattern of girls' work being "marked up." . . . Teachers are said to reward "organisational skills, good behaviour and compliance" rather than objectively marking pupils' work. (N.p.)

These findings will be controversial with many people including educators. It is discouraging to think that biases based on gender could find a way into our school system. We expect fairness and consistency to be foundational in our society; yet, *we don't expect it to occur in our classrooms*. Some stakeholders may feel defensive about this unacceptable situation, and so our regional studies delved into this issue at considerable length by assessing gender bias for students from grade *one through to university*.

In our region's *mathematics* tests, male students scored higher on grades three, six, and nine system tests at both the *Acceptable Standard* and *Standard of Excellence*. When teachers were required to report on student report cards, their *classroom assessments* of student achievement in grades one through nine, more males were assessed as functioning *below grade level in every grade*. In these evaluations, students' final marks were based exclusively on the teachers' assessment without knowing how students performed on our standardized tests, because these system tests were given in the final week of the school year after report cards were already completed.

Near the end of grade nine, students *self-selected* a mathematics stream for senior high school which would lead to university programming. Unfortunately for male students, programming decisions are made in April for next September but, since system tests occur at the end of June, *classroom marks weigh heavily in decisions*. Students and their parents did not receive their grade nine system test results until the end of September, well after they had begun their grade ten course. Participation rates in the grade ten, *upper stream mathematics course* favored females even though males demonstrated higher proficiency on the system tests.

This aspect of the study is significant because grade ten programming is the first screen in choosing a career. Enrolling in the lower stream mathematics course curtails qualification for university acceptance and, coincidentally, career aspirations. Mathematics is a significant *gate-keeper into the world of work* and the screening process, influenced by the biases as are presented, is eliminating many males from contending.

Experiencing a disadvantage in *gaining placement* in the upper stream mathematics course, male students continue to experience a negative bias further limiting their potential for scholarships and acceptance by universities. In this study, school-awarded marks and examination marks each count for 50 percent of the final course mark, and more female students received *the Standard of Excellence* from the *school-awarded marks* while more males received this high standard on the diploma examination. *This pattern of assessment was consistent over a period of seven consecutive semesters.*

From a broader perspective of examining all courses in English, mathematics, sciences, and social studies, the analysis underscores an advantage for female students. *Aggregating seven consecutive semesters* across these courses—seventy tests—females received *almost double* the "A" marks received by males from teachers' *class marks*—that is, females received 13.3 percent of "A's" while 6.7 percent of males received "A's." *Diploma Examination marks* told a different story as male students scoring "A" marks averaged 8.7 percent while females were at 9.0 percent. When combining, and weighing both sets of marks equally, females held a substantial advantage gleaned from their high set of classroom marks.

Considering only the *upper stream courses*, which are critical determinants for accessing universities, *school level* "A" marks were 66 percent more frequent than *diploma examination* "A" marks, which demonstrates the high level of *grade inflation* for these important subjects. *Classroom* level "A" marks favored females by 11.4 percent, while *examination* "A" marks favored males by 8.1 percent. Since the data set demonstrates significant grade inflation at the school level, females receive substantial advantage in securing scholarships and placements into prestigious universities.

A superintendent, who became aware of these disturbing trends, undertook a study in his school district. He tracked all student marks by gender as they progressed through high school, and monitored trends as students went from one teacher gender to the other. His review revealed a disturbing fact.

Female students going from a grade where the teacher was a female to a grade where the teacher was a male experienced a *bump up* in their marks. While males progressing from a male to a female teacher also benefited, the bump up was not significant. When the superintendent apprised his principals with these findings, he was greatly disturbed by their response. They readily acknowledged the unfair situation and referred to it as the "halter-top effect." This district was home to a hippie remnant and this sad revelation underscores how bias can intervene in efforts to ensure fairness for students.

The advantage for female students evident in the regional study also translated into a 2007 *Stats Can* national report for Canada entitled "Why are Most University Students Women" (https://www150.statcan.gc.ca/n1/daily-quotidien/070920/dq070920b-eng.htm). This study found that

> the gap in university attendance is largely associated with differences in academic performance and study habits at the age of 15, parental expectations, and other characteristics of men and women. . . . Weaker academic performance among men accounted for almost one-half (45%) of the gap. Specifically, young men had lower overall school marks at age 15 and had poorer performance on a standardized reading test. . . . In the 2001 Census, universities had clearly become the domain of women, as they made up 58 percent of all graduates. . . . We find the differences in the characteristics of boys and girls account for more than three quarters (76.8%) of the gap in university participation. In order of importance, the main factors are differences in school marks at age 15 (31.8%). (N.p.)

The *school mark* is the leading contributor for answering the question, "Why are most university students women?" The message in this study is made more significant when we factor in that most Canadian students progressing from high school to university submit marks only generated by their teachers. In other words, most provinces do not have exit examinations in grade twelve which counterbalance the biased marks from teachers. The "weaker academic performance among men" is a significant factor given the evidence that demonstrates *their marks are impacted negatively by noncompliant behaviors.*

When the school system does not implement *standardized testing accompanied by anonymous marking,* the male gender is disadvantaged when seeking entry into universities. *York University* in Ontario already is reporting their enrollment at 70 percent female, which is significant because Ontario suffers from the highest levels of grade inflation in Canada. *The higher is the rate of grade inflation, the greater is the potential for female acceptance into universities because of their more compliant school behaviors.*

This disadvantage is corroborated in the United States by another study released in an October 2006 article in the *American School Board Journal,* where the authors suggested what administrators might find when examining their districts (http://texasedequity.blogspot.com/2006/10/learning-and-gender_17.html):

> Boys, they'll probably notice, make up 80 to 90 percent of the district's discipline referrals, 70 percent of learning-disabled children, and at least two-thirds of the children on behavioral medication. They'll probably find that boys earn two-thirds of the Ds and Fs in the district, but less than half the As. (N.p.)

Further, Cummon (2018) reported on his American review stating,

> Girls tend to receive lower test scores relative to their school grades, whereas boys receive higher test scores relative to their school grades. There are multiple conjectures to explain this discrepancy in mean gender differences between tests and grades (e.g., on average, girls behave better, which gives them an advantage in grades). (N.p.)

In our regional study, three times as many male students were coded with moderate or severe disabilities, and two times more with mild or moderate disabilities. At the same time, males coded with different types of disabilities generally *tended to outperform* coded females when teachers assessed their grade level of achievement. *In other words, more male students were identified as "special needs" but assessed as demonstrating higher achievement by teachers.* An obvious question is whether all of these males should have been coded or were they being boys in a female-dominated world? Definitely, *caring about fairness for boys and girls specifically is a transformational issue for education.*

Grade inflation resulting from low standards or expectations that teachers have of their students is a significant problem. Students and their parents receive false information about how well the academic curriculum is learned. This misleading information instills a *false sense of security* in students who then lose some of their motivation for contributing their best effort. Ultimately, taxpayers are robbed from having students prepared to a level that will maximize potential.

A second message follows the first but that should increase the trepidation we have toward the effectiveness of our school system. *Grade inflation is not equally applied across all students but, rather, favors the female gender with an advantage in securing awards, scholarships, and placement in prestigious university programs.* This disadvantage toward males may be unfair, but it is disregarded and kept hidden from public scrutiny because educators do not want to lose the confidence of taxpayers and their government representatives.

For teachers and their unions, the alternative to resolving this unfairness is unpalatable acquiescence to the use of *standardized testing* where individual control over construction of the assessment is lost and *students' anonymity* is ensured. Perhaps of even greater importance is that any use of standardized testing permits higher levels of accountability for results, and such increased transparency for system quality has implications not only for the educators but also the politicians responsible for the school system.

This assumes that society does not shrug an apathetic and disengaged shoulder, saying, "That's life, nobody said that it is going to be fair!" Such reasoning would go on to say, "After all, we have operated with this situation for generations and many educators were aware of the effect but never made a huge public issue about it, so why now?"

Why now? Because our forefathers made decisions in the past with the knowledge that was available to them. No large-scale, reliable database existed to inform decisions. Why now? Because the public today demands action in the face of evidence and transparency, when accountability issues are at stake. Until recently, the educator's public creed was, "students first" and "we are in this for the kids." If this remains true and has meaning, then the rules related to fairness will have to change.

KEY POINTS

- Standardized tests are any test given to two or more students.
- Teachers believe in standardized testing because they use these almost every day.
- Many teachers are opposed to standardized testing because they are given to more than one class and provide for comparison of results.
- Grade level of achievement assessments from teachers balances standardized testing.
- Grade inflation is rampant partly because students and parents feel good about higher marks.

- Grade inflation is not equally applied across students but favors female students.
- Many universities are predominantly (more than two-thirds) female.
- OECD's PISA tests confirm the universality of the female advantage.
- Standardized testing accompanied by anonymous marking is a successful strategy for reducing grade inflation.

Chapter 6

The Males' Ship Is Listing Badly

The previous chapter informs us how inconsistent marking by classroom teachers of their students' work is a significant problem with *assessments generally skewed upward* creating a condition referred to as *grade inflation*. Equally problematic is the propensity for teachers to allow biases, most notably students' compliant behaviors, to influence their marking, which advantages female students when school systems dispense awards and scholarships. Marks are also a student's currency for gaining entry into university programs, and the *grade inflation advantage enjoyed by female students ensures more are successful with their applications*.

The politically correct response, if the situation was reversed, would produce strong denunciations that this situation is unfair; which it would be. Millennia of male domination justify efforts at ensuring equal opportunity and rights for females; and these have occurred. However, *the issue requiring attention in our education system is whether assessments of learning should be conflated with social and cultural factors such as compliant behavior, neatness in work, minority status, and so on.*

Permitting these types of biases to influence assessments of learning, which our evidence corroborates for male students in the schools' female-dominated workplace, *is unfair*. There are other strategies, such as affirmative action where formulae are transparently utilized, which can adjust a legitimate cultural need. *The current injustice penalizes male students unfairly with lifelong consequences and is a reverse discrimination requiring public debate.* However, a thoughtful discussion cannot occur until the matter is *exposed for public scrutiny and discussion*, which was the purpose of the previous chapter.

POSTSECONDARY BLOCKAGE

A key concern occurs when students graduate from high school and endeavor to pursue their career interest. Many males are previously culled prior to senior high school programming by unfair assessments negatively influenced by their behavior. Then, ongoing unfair assessments through high school programs further mitigated successful applications into postsecondary opportunities, which impact negatively on fulfilling career choices and potential earnings. In other words, many male students are penalized in school perpetuating lifelong injustice.

Mounting evidence demonstrates the extent to which unfairness is now several decades old. In Canada, for example, a Statscan report in 2013/14 chronicles a trend as well as a partial assessment of why this is occurring: (https://www150.statcan.gc.ca/n1/pub/89-503-x/2010001/article/11542-eng.htm).

Women have progressed considerably in terms of education and schooling over the past few decades. Just twenty years ago, a smaller percentage of women than men aged twenty-five to fifty-four had a postsecondary education. Today, the situation is completely different. Education indicators show that women generally do better than men. This gap in favor of women is even noticeable at a young age, since girls often get better marks than boys in elementary and secondary school (n.p.).

This report affirms a message regarding which gender receives higher marks from their classroom teachers. This analysis, however, does not delve into the next step and compare class marks with standardized assessments utilizing anonymous marking, which is the critical analysis necessary for understanding gender bias. Figure 6.1 portrays how this unchecked grade inflation in Canada's classrooms has translated into a gender advantage for females in every province by 2009 (https://www150.statcan.gc.ca/n1/pub/89-503-x/2010001/article/11542/c-g/c-g002-eng.htm).

A noteworthy demographic demonstrated in this 2009 chart (figure 6.1) is the relative parity evident in Alberta, the bastion in Canada of standardized testing and anonymous marking. Despite claims that the province's oil patch

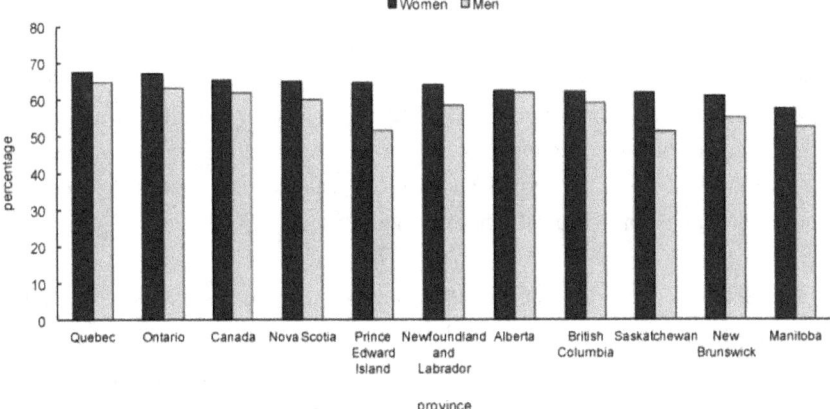

Figure 6.1   Percentage of Women and Men with a Postsecondary Degree, by Province, 2009.

lures many males away from postsecondary institutions, Alberta offers the greatest parity in citizens holding a degree. This province has a history of recording the lowest levels of grade inflation across the nation: an outcome attributed to the use of standardized assessments in grades three, six, nine, and twelve. *These assessments serve as a check and balance in the school system so that educators know whether they are allowing classroom standards to creep downward, resulting in grade inflation.*

On the other hand, two provinces—Saskatchewan and Prince Edward Island—did not use any form of provincial testing, and the disparity between male and female degree holders is greater than 10 percent: more than double the percentages of all other provinces. These provinces have a history of students receiving high-class marks from their teachers while faring less well on national and international assessments. The gender disparity evident in figure 6.1 provides credence to our concern regarding female students benefiting with higher marks from classroom teachers.

Pratt (2011) provides additional insight into this phenomenon in an interview with Dan Seneker, manager of undergraduate recruitment at the University of Saskatchewan in Saskatoon, regarding his views on provincial diploma examinations:

> He has heard over the years from lots of Alberta parents concerned that their kids are at a disadvantage in competing for spots in top faculties and for

scholarship money because they are held to a higher standard with the diploma exams. The exams so often pull down a student's marks that Alberta students are less likely to graduate with an A average. Of course, there are always kids who do brilliantly on exams and good for them. In lots of cases, the exams—that no other students in the country have to write—work to lower a mark of lots of smart kids even by a few points and that can make an enormous difference—whether you get into medical school or engineering. (N.p.)

These words from the recruitment manager are consistent with the messages in the previous chapter related to grade inflation. Diploma examinations are *presented as a culprit* in holding Alberta graduates from gaining entry into universities; yet, these examination questions are prepared annually by teams of teachers from across the province under the supervision of a full-time manager; have all questions thoroughly vetted through field testing in classrooms of students to reduce bias and confusion; and are marked by at least two teachers with the writers' identity kept *anonymous*.

A nugget for understanding the grade inflation problem is evident in the manager's words, "He has heard over the years from lots of Alberta parents concerned that their kids are at a disadvantage in competing for spots in top faculties and for scholarship money because they are held to a higher standard with the diploma exams." *Simply, if marks are getting too low within an organization such as a school, school district, or province for entry into university, resolve the issue by lowering standards.* An organization's students will win if it inflates students' grades more. If undetected, such *fraudulent* activity works! Inflating students' grades is not legally punished: at least not yet.

The Province of Ontario provides an example of how their education system responded to limited spaces in universities. According to a "Making the Grade" report in the University of Queen's Journal on September 19, 2008, 90 percent of Ontario's students had a "B" average or greater and 60 percent applying for university had an "A" average (Woods 2008). Teachers were making certain that their students would get a chance to qualify for the shortage of seats and the reporter concluded that "The number of 'A' students isn't growing because people are getting smarter. Rather, academic standards have declined so it is easier to get an 'A' than ever before—a phenomenon known as grade inflation" (n.p.).

Forgotten in this analysis is that grade inflation is not equally occurring across all students. There are winners and losers because *classroom assessments lack the quality of system examinations* thereby allowing bias to creep into the process resulting in unfairness. Males are the victims in the flawed process of relying exclusively on classroom assessments, and *governments choosing to ignore the outcomes are the villains in their unfair treatment of male students.*

Pratt's article goes on to say, "Alberta can be proud that it holds students to a higher standard. Students here are marked harder, and those that manage to go on to postsecondary do better—that is, their marks don't drop as much at university, Seneker found" (n.p.). In other words, Alberta's students' achievement is more closely aligned with expectations of Saskatchewan universities' expectations for students entering programs, which should be the basis upon which the selections should be determined.

Attempting to understand the relatively recent turnabout in gender participation in university, as documented in figure 6.1, motivated Karis (2011) to examine the issue regarding male students constantly taught by a female teacher:

> At UVic [University of Victoria, British Columbia], 57.1 per cent of current undergraduate students are female and 42.9 per cent are male, according to Tony Eder, a director for UVic's Institutional Planning and Analysis. . . . This trend is escalated by an increasing number of males dropping out of PSIs [Post-Secondary Institutions] worldwide. Eder explains that the exact number is difficult to track because there is no way of concluding whether it is a leave of absence or a more permanent decision.
>
> Jamie Cassels, UVic's Vice-President Academic and Provost, believes there's not yet an answer for this phenomenon. "For almost 10 years, it's been like that: a female population that is at about 60 per cent versus 40 per cent for males. And it varies. It's interesting that it's not getting worse. The question for me is, is it even a problem? If it is a problem, are there barriers and problems at the university level or is it happening somewhere else?"
>
> One theory suggests the gap between males and females begins in elementary school due to the fact that the vast majority of elementary teachers are female, and the mentoring position teachers have at such a young age. . . . Teaching is female-oriented and that means a lot of boys don't have role models in the education system. They lose motivation to go further. (N.p.)

Karis' conclusion provides only one theory to explain the gender gap in university, and the theory that there exists a paucity of male role models in our school system is consistent with our explanation.

Drolet (2007) examined this problem of gender gap and proffered his perspective. The gender gap is a fact in most OECD countries, but he wonders whether this is just an interesting sociological phenomenon, or a symptom of some deeper problem for males? At this point, he concludes that no one is quite sure, and references an American researcher, Rob Crosnoe, a social psychologist at the University of Texas at Austin, who observes a concern also consistent with this book's theme.

> But there's a conundrum: while girls are getting better grades overall in math and science classes, boys are doing better on standardized tests. People are still trying to figure out what's going on there. It could mean that the grades that girls are getting in math and science reflect lots of different things, like behaviour and effort and things that aren't reflected in a standardized test.
>
> But in the globalized knowledge economy, a lack of education is a serious handicap. Fully 82 percent of Canadian males aged 18 to 21 are not in university, and men are less prepared than women are for the new economy, say some analysts. . . .
>
> This is an international phenomenon: the 2006 edition of the OECD's Education at a Glance says postsecondary graduation rates for girls exceed those for boys in 19 out of 22 OECD countries. (N.p.)

Conflating *behavior with learning* for deriving final marks about academic achievement is the critical issue. When a student is being assessed on the ability to multiply fractions or understand meanings from a paragraph, should the mark be influenced by their classroom behavior? One senior administrator contributed his personal feelings of bias when conducting assessments of students' work when he was a classroom teacher. His explanation of the insidious nature of bias was evident with his illustration of experience in marking work submitted by students who were the children of the city's mayor, the police chief, the town drunk, a cousin, a neighbor, and so on.

His examples demonstrate the importance of *anonymous marking* and how this contributes to fairness. Seldom do teachers ensure that assignments are marked completely anonymously and, indeed, even less likely does a teacher in one school exchange assignments with one from another school in order to ensure total anonymity. Parents should request whether this strategy was employed whenever they are conferencing with their child's teacher.

PUBLIC'S FOCUS ON GENDER IMBALANCE

Fortunately, media attention regarding gender imbalance in postsecondary institutions is increasing, and Macleans Magazine (August 12, 2013) published a list of Canadian institutions with more than 66 percent female students:

1. Mount Saint Vincent University, Halifax 75%
2. NSCAD University, Halifax 74%
3. Université du Québec en Outaouais, Gatineau, Que. 71%
4. Alberta College of Art + Design, Calgary 70%
5. Université du Québec à Rimouski, Rimouski, Que. 70%
6. Université Sainte-Anne, Church Point, N.S. 70%
7. Emily Carr University of Art + Design, Vancouver 69%
8. OCAD University, Toronto 69%
9. Brandon University, Brandon, Man. 68%
10. Nipissing University, North Bay, Ont. 68%
11. St. Thomas University, Fredericton, N.B. 68%

Macleans identified one institution—Royal Military College of Canada, Kingston, Ont.—with more than two-thirds male enrollment at 82 percent.

The U.S. media is also attentive to the shifting gender enrollment for colleges and universities. Rocheleau (2016) reported that women accounted for 55 percent of undergraduates enrolled at four-year colleges in the United States as of fall 2014. *His report concludes that the gap will continue to grow in coming years*, according to some projections and that some experts say, "The higher incidence of behavioral and school disciplinary problems among boys may be a factor" (n.p.). This statement about behavior is wide open to interpretation but is at the crux of the matter in this book.

Pew Research Center researchers, Lopez and Gonzalez-Barrera (2014), examined the trend of high school completers enrolled in college for 1994 and 2012.

- Among Hispanics, males increased from 52 to 62 percent but females increased from 52 to 76 percent. A female over male net increase of 14 percent.

- Among Blacks, males increased from 56 to 57 percent but females increased from 48 to 69 percent. A female over male net increase of 20 percent.
- Among Whites, males remained the same at 62 percent but females increased from 66 to 72 percent. A female over male net increase of 6 percent.
- Among Asians, males increased from 82 to 83 percent but females increased from 81 to 86 percent. A female over male net increase of 4 percent. (N.p.)

In each of these four groupings, the percentage of females enrolling outstripped the males.

Marcus (2017) explored this gender divide further and explained:

Where men once went to college in proportions far higher than women—58 percent to 42 percent as recently as the 1970s—the ratio has now almost exactly reversed. This fall, women will comprise more than 56 percent of students on campuses nationwide, according to the U.S. Department of Education. Some 2.2 million fewer men than women will be enrolled in college this year. And the trend shows no sign of abating. By 2026, the department estimates, 57 percent of college students will be women. (N.p.)

The similar trend of females enrolling in postsecondary schooling at greater rates than males is also a concern in the United Kingdom. Ratcliffe (2013) reported that in 2010–2011, there were more female (55 percent) than male full-time undergraduates (45 percent) enrolled at university—a trend which he suggested shows no sign of shrinking.

Similarly, Australia reports that the gender gap among domestic students has widened to almost 20 percent—up from 16.2 percent a decade ago—and Martin (2015) reported that a leading education expert is calling for the lack of men at university to be considered an equity issue. This reporter quotes an education expert who claims that *"the imbalance began in school years. We have got a national issue to face up to, and that is particularly in middle and secondary [schooling]. Young men are not doing as well as they should"* (n.p.).

This pattern of females being the dominant group in postsecondary education is consistent across Europe, with one exception. According to Eurostat's report of 2013, more than 19.6 million students were in attendance across the continent comprised of approximately 9 million males and 10.7 million females. Out of the thirty-four countries in Europe, only Germany reported a majority of male students (https://ec.europa.eu/eurostat/documents/3217494/6856423/KS-05-14-073-EN-N/742aee45-4085-4dac-9e2e-9ed7e9501f23).

There is not a right or wrong answer regarding gender participation in postsecondary schooling; however, a significant cultural shift toward female participation is evident. Factors bringing about this shift are complex and impossible to calculate, but it is impossible to ignore the research contained within these pages demonstrating the impact of having males taught almost exclusively in the early grades by female teachers and the biases teachers bring to one of their primary tasks of assessing student learning.

There can be no equivocation, however, that ignoring this shift is as unfair as are many biases existing with females. Consequences emanating from the school system, where many male children are stifled from achieving their potential, is not in society's best interests.

A dramatically decreasing male-teacher problem is exacerbating the current unfairness. Teacher hiring in North America follows a free-market principle. People who want to pursue a career in education register for training programs, graduate, and enter the market seeking employment where they hope to be hired. Prospective employers examine credentials and attempt to match these with their needs.

Gender may be one of these needs, but the prevailing culture discourages specifying it. In the United States, the National Center for Education Information reported in 2005 that 82 percent of public school teachers were female. This percentage was up from 69 percent in 1986 and 74 percent in 1996. In Canada, almost three-quarters of teachers are female (Dueck, 2017).

The UK's *Daily Mail* (https://www.dailymail.co.uk/news/article-1324905/Pupils-make-effort-male-teachers-seen-fair.html) on November 13, 2010, summarized the concern:

Pupils try harder for male teachers, according to an official study.

They make more effort to please them, display greater self-esteem and are more likely to believe they are being treated fairly.

With the number of male secondary school teachers also dwindling, it is feared that some youngsters could go throughout their entire education without experiencing the benefits of being taught by a man.

The findings are particularly significant as more than a quarter of primary schools do not have a single male teacher.

A recent study by Kent University found that women teachers are holding back boys by reprimanding them for typically male behaviour.

They are reinforcing stereotypes that boys are "silly" in class and refuse to "sit nicely like the girls" and are more likely to indulge in pranks.

Fair treatment for all individuals is a critical hallmark of our democratic society, and we should stand in one accord when the school system denies fairness to a group of students, in this instance males. *The remedy for achieving fairness requires standardized testing accompanied by anonymous marking.* The previous chapter, however, recorded the opposition educators and their representatives have toward these system tests.

KEY POINTS

- Marks are a student's currency for gaining entry into university programs.
- The current injustice penalizes male students unfairly with lifelong consequences.
- Female grade inflation provides a significant advantage for entry into post-secondary in all provinces except Alberta, the bastion of standardized testing and anonymous marking.
- The gender gap is a fact in most OECD countries.
- A dramatically decreasing male-teacher problem is exacerbating the current unfairness.

Chapter 7

Teacher Pay

How well workers are paid is a perennial issue especially for those involved in the public sector where salaries are derived from the public purse. Educator salaries frequently garner attention because their work year is significantly different from virtually all other workers and their pay is derived from the public purse. This issue of pay must be discussed because attracting competent workers into the profession is an important factor in a nation's long-term success. When students *learn well*, they have greater potential to *live well*.

Pay scale data from around the world usually is several years out of date because this research is infrequently undertaken. Brookings (https://www.brookings.edu/blog/brown-center-chalkboard/2016/06/20/teacher-pay-around-the-world/) in figure 7.1 identified the highest levels of teachers' pay for 2013 showing Canada at 4th and the United States at 27th (Note: OECD is the average of all countries associated with the Organization for Economic Cooperation and Development). Comparatively speaking, *Canadian teachers are well paid and the U.S. teachers are not*. This chart provides for an unambiguous comparison.

POWER POINT #14

Figure 7.1 indicates why Canadian teachers seldom make salary their primary bargaining issue, choosing, instead, to focus on class size, or less work as their target. The situation across the United States is entirely different. The U.S. surveys of teachers and parents annually (https://pdkpoll.org/wp-

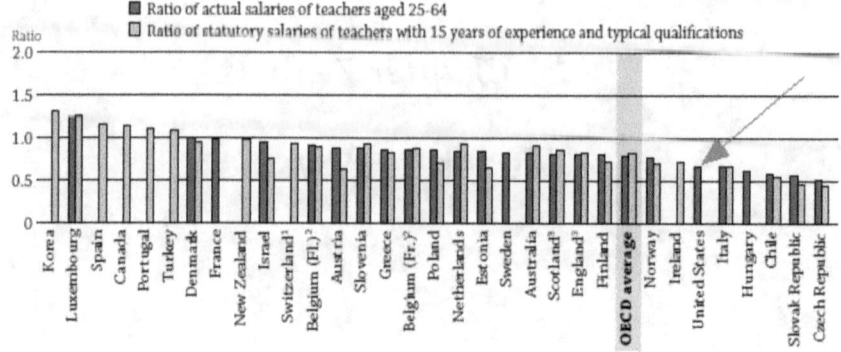

Figure 7.1 Teachers' Salaries Relative to Earnings for Similarly Educated Workers (2013).

content/uploads/2020/05/pdkpoll51-2019.pdf) provide readers with fascinating results in 2019.

Education is seldom cut-and-dried to the extent that other comparisons frequently are necessary. For example, the annual survey of U.S. teachers and parents in 2019 reported:

- 60% of teachers say they're unfairly paid, and 55% say they'd vote to go on strike for higher pay. (K4)
- Seventy-five percent of teachers say the schools in their community are underfunded. (K4)
- A majority of teachers—55%—would not want their child to follow them into the profession. (K4)
- Americans saying the public schools in their community are underfunded. (K3)
- 74% of parents and 71% of all adults say they would support a strike by teachers in their community for higher pay. (K4)

American teachers' salaries are well below what is the standard for other wealthy countries especially when considering how much money the United States spent for education. According to https://nces.ed.gov/programs/coe/indicator_cmd.asp spending for education in 2016 and using constant 2018 U.S. dollars, *funding per student* in various countries is (1) Luxembourg: $20,400, (2) Switzerland: $15,000, (5) US: $13,600, (11) UK: $11,600, (13) Canada: $11,100, and OECD average is $9,800. U.S. taxpayers are very generous to their school system despite disturbing test results.

The 2018 PISA test results reported at https://i2.wp.com/factsmaps.com/wp-content/uploads/2019/12/pisa-2018.png provide the *average score* of mathematics, science, and reading for fifteen-year-old students in seventy-seven countries. A few of these scores are listed below with that country's education expenditures indicated numerically in bolded numbers.

1) China @578.7 (However, only four cities participate: a concession to have this country participate)
8) Canada @ 516.7
13) United Kingdom @503.7
25) United States @ 495.0
26) France @ 493.7
30) Russia @ 487.3
35) Luxembourg @ 476.7

Specifically, the American scores for each test placed their students at 13th in reading, 18th in science, and 37th in mathematics while, in Canada, students placed 6th in reading, 8th in science, and 12th in mathematics. *These lower mathematics results for both North American nations should lead politicians to re-think their region's commitment to the Discovery Learning teaching methodology.*

Barber and Mourshed (2005) remind us about the relationship between learning and teaching:

> The quality of an education system cannot exceed the quality of its teachers. The evidence that getting the right people to become teachers is critical to high performance is both anecdotal and statistical. . . .
>
> The top-performing systems we studied recruit their teachers from the top-third of each cohort graduate from their school system. . . .
>
> Conversely, lower-performing school systems rarely attract the right people into teaching. The New Commission on the Skills of the American Workforce observes that, "We are now recruiting our teachers from the bottom-third of high school students going to college . . . it is simply not possible for students to graduate [with the skills they will need] . . . unless their teachers have the knowledge and skills we want our children to have." (p.16)

This alarming commentary coupled with the OECD's portrait in figure 7.1 provides credible evidence for American teachers' demands for higher wages. Their argument, however, would be a double-edged sword because they would have acknowledged that their original level of skill entering university is associated with American students' low level of performance. Nevertheless, dramatic reform in the American education system is required and increased salary for teachers is a logical beginning point. However, from where should the money come when the American taxpayer is already so generous?

Over time, public sector organizations allow trends in misspending which waste valuable resources. A sport stadium is one stark contrast between Canadian and American high schools. As a young footballer traveling from a BC high school to a small American high school, we were in awe at the stadium hosting our game. Overall, American schools have produced great athletes but fewer well-educated students.

Education administrators attempted to improve student achievement by releasing the home from its responsibility to feed their child. Breakfast and lunch programs are wide spread but has the taxpayer received the stated benefits from this socialistic program? By 1996, school lunch and breakfast programs grew to 4.8 percent of total school spending (https://www.epi.org/publication/books_wheremoneyes/).

Identifying more students for special education is another strategy in substantiating requests for more funding. Heasley (2018) reports that 6.7 million students with disabilities were enrolled in classrooms across the country during the 2015–2016 school year, accounting for 13.2 percent of all students. Is identifying almost one in seven students as special needs realistic or have administrators lowered standards to capture more students? In our work with a provincial team of auditors, we found a tendency to expand the identifiers so that more students qualified for special needs.

Perhaps the greatest concern with wasted spending comes from our comparison of administrative units in the United States and Canada. The U.S. education system is organized into approximately 13,500 school districts (https://nces.ed.gov/programs/digest/d12/tables/dt12_098.asp) which is approximately 37.3 times as many as Canada's 362. Our comparison reveals an actual population variance of approximately nine Americans for every Canadian. In other words, proportionally, *the U.S. school system operates with more than four times as many school districts*; however, test results lag far behind Canada.

These additional administrative units require a superintendent and administrators of lesser rank as well as business officials and support workers. They also require office space, buildings, and equipment. The duplication of administrative costs relative to the Canadian education system is significant.

Some American administrators may object to this comparison; however, Canada's situation is compounded by having two official languages requiring separate schools and districts across the country. Further, six of the thirteen p rovinces and territories still allow faith-based school boards to be supported with tax money which add complexity to the official languages component with its requirement to provide for two official religious affiliations. These constitutional requirements necessitate many additional school systems.

Concern with the cost of these administrative units caused the Goldwater Institute (https://www.heritage.org/education/commentary/goldwater-institute-school-districts-waste-money-could-pay-teachers) to conduct an audit in Arizona for district officials wherein:

> The superintendent of Sunnyside Unified School District makes more than six times what the average teacher in the district earns. In Tucson, it's more than five times the average teacher pay. The numbers are similar for many other districts, from Paradise Valley to Buckeye. (N.p.)

Of course, superintendents respond to this type of comparison by referencing their length of tenure which averages approximately six years (https://www.educationdive.com/news/report-average-superintendent-tenure-about-6-years/523089/). Yes, their employment may be tenuous but leaving a position does not necessitate leaving their profession.

Substantial savings through *school district consolidation* release funds sufficient to increase teacher wages commensurate with other sector jobs. Increasing the quality of intake will provide a higher quality of student achievement. Taxpayers do not need to pay more but should expect that the school system will be more efficient, including a re-examination of a teacher's work year.

TEACHERS' WORK SCHEDULE

This discussion about the teachers' work schedule is relevant because teachers frequently bemoan their levels of pay in comparison with other professions. They refer to an annual salary but *neglect to consider their personal benefits of almost three months' annual vacation.* Equally significant is the time of year when these vacations occur. Children are not the only ones who enjoy the warm and sunny days of summer. What value should teachers assign to the privilege of having vacations during "prime time," whether these occur during seasons of best weather or periods encompassing major holidays?

Therefore, when workers compare annual salaries, and vacation time, these benefits must be factored into the calculation. Generally speaking, teachers benefit from approximately two additional months of annual vacation compared to the average person in the workforce who receives about three weeks a year. This additional vacation equates to approximately a 15 percent perk which is a significant amount of money. Any discussion of salary which ignores this cost factor is meaningless.

There is a myriad of additional benefits in a typical teacher salary package. Pensions, paid sick leave, discretionary days, preparation time as well as many other types of releases from work, both paid and unpaid, *can cost taxpayers close to 25 percent of the annual salary.* When private sector workers reference these additional benefits, they are frequently confronted by defensive teachers; however, it is reasonable to consider that all of these benefits, including the lengthy vacation period, results in a salary "bump" of approximately 40 percent above the publicized salary. An annual *salary* of $80,000 is *valued at* approximately $112,000.

School districts that are serious about reform need to take the true teacher's cost into consideration, if they have made student achievement their primary goal. Some districts are now lengthening the school year for students who are struggling with academic success. *The lengthy vacation period, enshrined in union agreements, is now an impediment to reform because it is considered an entitlement.* As a consequence, the school district has to reduce services, increase taxes, or both in order to maintain the status quo in a world of accelerating costs.

CURRENT PAY BONUSES ARE WRONGHEADED

The current model for paying teachers is outdated because it omits taking results into consideration when determining an appropriate salary for the teacher. However, we must still debunk another pernicious idea in both Canada and the United States that plagues the system: paying teachers for getting older and acquiring more education also perpetuates ineffectiveness. *These two aspects have been in use for decades and have cost taxpayers large sums of money, but without justification.* Indeed, the focus contributed to less than excellent service for our children because teachers are rewarded for things that do not yield results.

Educators are like other humans and respond positively to extrinsic motivation such as pay. Extrinsic motivation in the form of money is already evident in the current payment program for teachers where they are incented to pursue additional degrees. Teachers readily pursue additional degrees in regions where these garner greater increases in salary. Additional remuneration is a sufficient incentive or bonus for many teachers to pursue a master's degree.

Hughes-Jones et al. (2006) also examined the issue of certification across three U.S. states and concluding that teachers' graduate degrees had no significant effect on student achievement. Buddin and Zamarro (2009) reviewed several criteria used for determining teacher pay and concluded that traditional teacher qualifications have little influence on classroom achievement. When analyzing student achievement data along with teacher qualifications, a five-year increase in teaching experience affected student achievement very little—*less than 1 percentage point*. Similarly, the level of education held by a teacher proved to have no effect on student achievement in the classroom.

Harris and Sass (2008) conducted their analysis of experience and certification indicating:

> Consistent with prior research, we find that estimates of teachers' contributions to student achievement or "value added" are at best weakly correlated with readily observable teacher characteristics like experience and attainment of advanced degrees, suggesting that other factors may be relatively more important in determining what makes a "good" teacher. (p.27)

Greene (2005) examined the certification issue labeling it a *myth*, and summarized his review regarding the importance of experience on teaching effectiveness. Teachers holding master's degrees did not produce higher student performance unless, at the high school, teachers with such a degree attained it in their subject specialty and not a degree in education generally.

Goe and Stickler (2008) similarly assessed the value of teachers pursuing additional certification and concluded that

> the effects associated with a teacher's possession of an advanced degree are strikingly counterintuitive, especially given the salary incentives offered to encourage teachers to pursue graduate degrees. Not only do recent empirical studies not find a substantial benefit for students of teachers with advanced degrees, but the majority of such studies also indicate that teachers with master's degrees and beyond may negatively influence their student's achievement. (p.3/4)

Roza and Miller (2009) differentiated the value of pursuing additional certification between subject areas and reported:

> On average, master's degrees in education bear no relation to student achievement. Master's degrees in math and science have been linked to improved student achievement in those subjects, but 90 percent of teachers' master's degrees are in education programs—a notoriously unfocused and process-dominated course of study. Because of the financial rewards associated with getting this degree, the education master's experienced the highest growth rate of all master's degrees between 1997 and 2007.
>
> So how much money is tied up in master's degrees? A 2007 study estimated that 2.1 percent of all current expenditures can be attributed to teacher compensation related to master's degrees.7 Seen another way, the master's bump costs the average school district $174 per pupil. (p.1/2)
>
> Divestment should be part of an effort to distribute compensation differently, in ways that offer greater benefit to students. Teachers currently finance their master's degree studies in anticipation of guaranteed financial returns, but if teachers anticipated higher pay based instead on enhanced ability to boost student achievement, their interests would be better aligned with those of their students. (p.4/5)

Kentucky's Blue Grass Institute (http://www.bipps.org/masters-degrees-many-say-dont-improve-teaching/) concluded: "It's clear that Kentucky's former requirement for teachers to obtain a master's degree wasn't translating into better student performance. . . . *The fact that teachers with master's degrees are no more effective in the classroom, on average, than their colleagues without advanced degrees is one of the most consistent findings in education research*" (n.p.).

We could go on at great length about these two issues and the rewards they bring. What is noteworthy is the absence of research that justifies the use of increased experience beyond the first couple of years and the acquisition of additional degrees as a reward for excellent service. Michael Bamesberger reported in the *Nebraskan* (2010) the conclusions of then U.S. secretary of education as well as those of an American philanthropist:

> In November (2010), U.S. Education Secretary Arne Duncan singled out the $8 billion spent on master's degree bonuses annually as wasteful, claiming there is "little evidence teachers with master's degrees improve students' achievement more than other teachers—with the possible exception of teachers who earn master's in math and science," according to a speech he gave to the American Enterprise Institute. Microsoft founder Bill Gates also came out in opposition to the bonuses, citing a University of Washington study in which master's degrees in education were found to bear no relation to student achievement. (N.p.)

While the issue of pay receives considerable attention in the United States, only a few Canadian studies are available. In 1997–1999, Canada tested students in reading, mathematics, and science and collected survey results from students and teachers. Using the teacher data and measuring the performance of students scoring at level three—the passing score—or better, Alberta's students scored the highest and had the greatest percentage of teachers with *less* than five years of postsecondary education. Coincidentally, Alberta's teachers had the lowest pay differential between a bachelor's and a second degree. By implication, therefore, teachers in Alberta were less motivated by degrees and experience than were teachers in other jurisdictions.

A few years later in 2007, the Council of Ministers' Education Canada undertook another review of student achievement in reading relative to teacher education levels (http://cmec.ca/Publications/Lists/Publications/Attachments/296/PCAP2007ReadingEN_Web.pdf). In this instance, students with teachers possessing a B.Ed. degree and some additional nonformal training scored significantly higher than did students in classes where the teacher possessed a graduate degree. One explanation for this counterintuitive result is that teachers with advanced degrees may become more interested in advancing their careers through administration rather than advancing skills for the classroom.

It is noteworthy that there is no research supporting the merits of the current system. Advanced university degrees are not producing improved student achievement. Why do we persist in funding a system that is not providing a return on investment? *Is it possible we are so enslaved to tradition that facts no longer guide our reasoning and logic in our decision making?* Is the alternative worrisome to unions because *value regarding job performance will be assessed based on student outcomes?*

With the evidence now available, it is indefensible to continue using the pay grid approach built on certification and years of experience. Jensen and Reichl (2011) get to the nub of the issue by reminding us of the folly in paying all teachers with the same experience *as though they are equally effective and improve at the same rate*. Teachers' unions' opposition toward pay-for-performance programs is fierce, and the more intense their opposition, the more clearheaded and wiser we need our politicians to be. A viable alternative is to increase teacher pay but incorporate a performance component which puts some pay at risk.

KEY POINTS

- Comparatively speaking, Canadian teachers are well paid and U.S. teachers are not.
- The United States stands fifth in the world for education funding.
- In the latest international assessments, Canada ranked 8th but United States ranked 25th.
- U.S. parents support higher teacher salaries.
- American teachers tend to come out of the bottom half of high school marks.
- The U.S. education system spends considerable funding on breakfast and special education; however, it also has a considerably greater number of school boards than does Canada.
- When teachers discuss their annual salaries, they overlook working less than forty weeks in a year, as well as an extensive benefits package.
- The long-standing practice of paying teachers for experience and additional education is not supported by research.

Chapter 8

Parents' Responsibility and Right

Parents' responsibility for *educating their child into the kind of adult they want them to become* is a fundamental point in this chapter. Many of our educational concerns emanate from the state interfering with this right. Education is a cornerstone of a child's development and future success, and most parents rely in part on an education program smoothing a way that prepares their child's successful transition to adulthood. Golston (2003) explains:

> The special relationship between parents and children must be reflected in the allocation of educational authority, and so must what I shall call the "expressive interest" of parents in raising their children in a manner consistent with their understanding of what gives meaning and value to life. . . . Among other implications, this schema means that civic concerns do not function as trumps in discussion of educational policy. (p.212)

A century ago, when social advocates promoted an enlarged role for governments in education found their efforts disregarded as an unwise, unwarranted, and unnatural overreach. Oregon, for example, attempted to require enrolling children between ages eight and sixteen in a public school thereby outlawing all private schools. In 1925, the Supreme Court intervened in this attempt by concluding that this initiative:

> Unreasonably interferes with the liberty of parents and guardians to direct the upbringing and education of children under their control. . . . The fundamental theory of Liberty upon which all governments in this Union repose excludes any general power of the state to standardize its children by forcing them to accept

instruction from public teachers only. The child is not the mere creature of the state; those who nurture him and direct his destiny have the right, coupled with the high duty, to recognize and prepare him for additional obligations. (Golston, p. 217)

This landmark ruling, as well as others related to this issue, codified into law the concepts of parental "right" and "high duty." Governments may require parents to ensure their child be educated, but *choices* remain in the parent's domain. The term "education" is not mentioned in the U.S. constitution likely because the "founders wanted most aspects of life managed by those who were closest to them, either by state or local government or by families, businesses, and other elements of civil society" (N.p.; Boaz, 2006).

Although the U.S. Constitution does not make education a fundamental right, the 14th Amendment requires that a state's public school system may not deny equal status to schooling. Boaz proceeds to point out that this amendment "prohibits any state from denying 'to any person within its jurisdiction the equal protection of the laws.' The equal protection clause clearly requires that all American citizens must be treated equally by the law" (n.p.).

Our critical point is that the state is not responsible for education, and parents have a legitimate right to declare and exercise their responsibility. Their tax dollars then fund state governments for *delivering* their child with an education which may be generalizable across states but is not necessarily common to all states. Hence, a recent effort by forty-six state governors at identifying a Common Core set of curriculum standards, which now continues with forty-one states.

AN ERA OF AMERICAN RELIGIOSITY

North American education in the mid-twentieth-century context included a religious component. Religiosity across the continent was at its height in those years, and "On a typical Sunday morning in the period from 1955–1958, almost half of all Americans were attending church—the highest percentage in U.S. history" (N.p.; Tucker, 1997). Billy Graham, one of the most recognizable names and faces, emerged out of this era. Similarly, 43% of Canadians born between 1934 and 1943 reported that they attended religious services at least once a month and 31% of the subsequent cohort (born 1944–1953) said they attended religious services monthly or more in the same year (n.p., Pew Research Center, "Canada's Changing Religious Landscape," 2013).

It was logical then that educational leadership incorporate some religious observances within the school's program:

- Bible reading featuring the Old Testament and the life of Jesus in the four gospels.
- Students recited the Lord's Prayer.
- Christmas was celebrated as the birth of the Christ Child.
- Gideons (volunteers from the business community) distributed free New Testaments to fifth grade students in their classrooms.
- Easter was celebrated for the death and resurrection of Jesus.
- School choirs and bands/orchestras featured many religious musicals.
- Students participated in Christian clubs (InterVarsity Christian Fellowship, etc.) during their time at school.
- Creationism was part of the curriculum.

After the 1960s, secularism increased and significant percentages of North American population became indifferent toward religion even to the extent of rejecting its teaching. Separation of church and state emerged as a dominant theme, and proponents argued that religious groups should not interfere with affairs of state and the state would not interfere in religious affairs. Many Christians chose accommodation and complacency in the face of a forceful secular opposition especially when, in the 1970s, church attendance began to decline.

Religion and education are linked through the centuries because understanding one of the world's oldest books, the Bible, required a level of reading ability, hence centuries of Catholic religious schools. We can argue that religion in the school system will never lose its relevance because its emphasis on the equality of all remains relevant to this day. Providing children with a moral compass for determining what is right or wrong provides balance for counteracting the many distracters facing our youth.

Grant (2014) summarized recent trends as a period when religiosity in the United States went through the midst of what might be called "The Great Decline" because previous declines in religion pale in comparison. The presence of established organized religion and the influence of Christianity, in particular, mirrored this decline in church attendance and the rise of a new religious value-laden secularism:

- Santa Claus became the main character of Christmas as "Happy Holidays" replaced "Merry Christmas."
- The crucifixion and resurrection were replaced by the Easter Bunny delivering colored eggs and candy.
- Bible reading and the Lord's Prayer disappeared and became illegal.
- Gideons were denied entry to the school and distributed Bibles on the public sidewalk.
- Some regions blocked Christian student clubs from meeting on campus.
- Evolution became the only taught and tolerated theory of origins.

Reaction to these aspects curtailing religious beliefs and practices is evident at both ends of the religious continuum. Many parents, for example, now step away from the public school and enroll their child(ren) in an independent or private school.

In Canada, where six of the thirteen provinces/territories still have Catholic schools, the Fraser Institute reported enrollment for independent schools (https://www.fraserinstitute.org/article/share-of-students-attending-independent-schools-increasing-in-every-province):

> What's most striking in the student enrolment data, given the overall decline in the school-aged population across Canada (excluding Alberta), is the proportion of students in each province that attend a government-run public school. In every province, a smaller share of students in 2014-15 attended a public school than did in 2000-01.
>
> The most dramatic shift was in British Columbia, which saw its share of enrolment in public schools drop from 90.6 per cent in 2000-01 to 86.8 per cent in 2014-15. Next was Quebec, which declined from 90.6 per cent to 87.6 per cent over the same period.
>
> The declining share of students attending government-run public schools is offset by an increasing number of parents choosing non-government options. Two main types exist in Canada—independent schools and homeschooling.
>
> Consider independent schools, which are independently owned and operated and home to diverse religious and pedagogical orientations such as Catholic, Christian non-Catholic, Jewish, Islamic or Montessori or arts-based education. In every province the share of students attending independent schools increased.

Independent schools in B.C. now enrol the largest share of any province's students (12.9 per cent) followed by Quebec (12.3 per cent) and Manitoba (7.9 per cent).

Even Ontario now has 6.1 per cent of students attending independent schools. This is a province, unlike the three just mentioned, where the government offers no support to independent schools, which means, like all of Atlantic Canada, parents bear the full costs of independent schooling. (N.p.)

Now, in most instances, parents for Christian education are sacrificing their personal finances to pay some or all tuition thereby ensuring a more holistic education for their child(ren). We emphasize that these parents are subsidizing government because their allotment of funds for schooling their child(ren) is going elsewhere.

Today, across the United States, traditionalists continue to confront the drive toward secularization. National education polling in the United States frequently includes questions about religion in public schools. A recent edition—https://news.gallup.com/poll/1612/education.aspx (n.p.)—provides the following polling results:

1) Making public school facilities available after school hours for use by student religious groups.
   Favor (%): 1999 @ *78*; 2001 @ *72*; 2014 @ *78*.
2) Allowing daily prayer to be spoken in the classroom.
   Favor (%): 1999 @ *70*; 2000 @ *68*; 2001@ *66*; 2014 @ *61*.
3) Allowing students to say prayers at graduation ceremonies as part of the official program. Favor (%): 1999 @ *83*; 2000 @ *77*; 2001 @ *75*; 2014 @ *74*.
4) Favor a constitutional amendment to allow voluntary prayer in public schools.
   1983 @ *81*; 1994 @ *73*; 2000 @ *74*; 2001 @ *78*; 2005 @ *76*.

The voices of the minority prevail.

In recent polling—https://pdkpoll.org/results/religious-study-in-school—Gallup reports 2019 results to a question related to Bible studies:

A recent trend toward including Bible studies in public high schools wins majority support in the 2019 PDK poll, with the provision that Bible studies should be an elective, not a requirement. Support is higher for including comparative religion classes, also as an elective. Specifically, among all adults, 58% say schools should offer Bible studies as an elective, and 6% say Bible studies should be required, totaling 64% who favor Bible classes in one of these formats. Sixty-eight percent of parents say the same, as do 58% of teachers. (p.11)

These polls reveal a gradual decline in religious studies but still have majority support in the U.S. parent population during these past two decades for religious activity in public schools. Presumably, many of these parents in the 2019 poll were born in the 1980s when, as children, they experienced considerable religious activity in their school.

Still, a startling question emerges: Why are the wishes of a *majority* not accommodated? The story begins with the *McCollum v. Board of Education*, 333 U.S. 203 (1948) ruling when the U.S. Supreme Court dealt with the matter of a state using its tax-supported public school system to aid *religious instruction*. This case was a test of the separation of church and state regarding education with a decision that religion and government can best work when each is left free from the other within its respective sphere (*McCollum v. Board of Education*, 333 U.S. 203 (1948)).

This ruling was reinforced in 1962 with the Supreme Court decision in *Engel v. Vitale*. It is summarized at https://www.uscourts.gov/educational-resources/educational-activities/facts-and-case-summary-engel-v-vitale. The majority ruled that

> school-sponsored prayer violates the Establishment Clause of the First Amendment. The majority stated that the provision allowing students to absent themselves from this activity did not make the law constitutional because the purpose of the First Amendment was to prevent government interference with religion. The majority noted that religion is very important to a vast majority of the American people. Since Americans adhere to a wide variety of beliefs, it is not appropriate for the government to endorse any particular belief system. The majority noted that wars, persecutions, and other destructive measures often arose in the past when the government involved itself in religious affairs. (N.p.)

Thus, in a *public school setting*, religious activity associated with particular religious ideology is not permitted.

QUALITY OF LIFE

Quality of life experiences is associated with religious teaching. The Bible, for example, is considered by many in the world as a *textbook* describing how citizens should live as well as interact with others. It outlines a set of beliefs that, if true, have implications for this life as well as the next. School libraries contain no equals and the Bible provides great relevance to today's social concerns:

- And as you wish that others would do to you, do so to them. (Lk. 6:31)
- Do not judge by appearances, but judge with right judgment. (John 7:24)
- For the whole law is fulfilled in one word: "You shall love your neighbor as yourself." (Gal. 5:14)
- This is my commandment, that you love one another as I have loved you. (John 15:12)
- Let all bitterness and wrath and anger and clamor and slander be put away from you, along with all malice. (Eph. 4:31)

Some might question whether our culture would actually benefit from such instruction? Official American crime statistics demonstrate a substantial decline; however, are they accurate? Gramlich (2020) responds to this question using Bureau of Justice Statistics (BJS) which counter assertions that crime across America is declining.

> In its annual survey, BJS asks crime victims whether they reported their crime to police or not. In 2019, only 40.9% of violent crimes and 32.5% of household property crimes were reported to authorities. BJS notes that there are a variety of reasons why crime might not be reported, including fear of reprisal or "getting the offender in trouble," a feeling that police "would not or could not do anything to help," or a belief that the crime is "a personal issue or too trivial to report."
>
> In 20 of 24 Gallup surveys conducted since 1993, at least 60% of U.S. adults have said there is more crime nationally than there was the year before, despite the generally downward trend in national violent and property crime rates during most of that period. (N.p.)

This national data, including the astounding evidence that the majority of criminal acts are not reported, begs the question of whether crime has actually decreased or has helplessness increased.

In addition to crime against one another, there is also considerable misuse of our own bodies which contravenes teaching in another Biblical law: "Do you not know that your body is a temple of the Holy Spirit within you, whom you have from God? You are not your own, for you were bought with a price. So glorify God in your body" (1 Cor. 6:19-20).

In the 1960s, student rebellion at school was confined generally to smoking cigarettes and drinking alcohol, while involvement with gangs trafficking illegal merchandise or substances was almost unknown. Indeed, a popular chant among teenagers was, "I don't smoke, and I don't chew, and I don't go with girls (boys) who do." There was, in that era, a significant percentage of young people attending churches where drinking alcohol and smoking were strongly discouraged.

In many regions, the law prohibited teenage use of these substances. Seldom were teachers required to deal with the residual effect of these substances and, when a student arrived at school under their influence, they were usually suspended. News of this punishment spread rapidly throughout the student body and acted as a deterrent to others.

The proliferation of television to the masses near the end of the 1950s helped erode the stigma of substance abuse known at that time. Capitalizing on this new "eye-gate," commercials featuring the rugged and handsome "Marlboro Man" inspired many adults, as well as children, to take up smoking. Other commercials, especially during sporting events, featured alcoholic beverages which introduced children to a new norm in adulthood. One father, when reminded of this commercial, related how he got out of his chair and stood as a visual barrier in front of the television when these commercials showed.

Faced with this new reality, school administrators backtracked from their abstinence perspective and established "smoking pits" for students during breaks in their daily schedule of classes. After all, students walked past smoke-filled staffrooms, and the legal community was already turning a blind eye to the mixed message this sent to teenagers regarding smoking habits.

Fast forwarding several decades to this generation of students reveals a significant problem. The American Lung Association (https://www.lung.org/quit-smoking/smoking-facts/tobacco-use-among-children) reported that "In 2015, 9.3% of high school students reported smoking cigarettes in the last

30 days, down 74% from 36.4% in 1997 when rates peaked after increasing throughout the first half of the 1990s" (n.p.). However, "Among high school students in 2015, the most prevalent forms of tobacco used were electronic cigarettes (16%), cigarettes (9.3%), cigars (8.6%) and hookah (7.2%)" (n.p.). A new era with students vaping has emerged.

Teenager alcohol use has also accelerated. Megan et al. (2011) revealed that approximately 75 percent of adolescents tried alcohol by the end of high school. This study identified media advertisements as the significant culprit in this disturbing trend, and that alcoholic brands used by teenagers were those used by companies with the highest advertising expenditures.

Hilliard (2019) reported how social media has impacted teen drug use:

Teens are uniquely vulnerable to the effects of what they see on social media, as this age group is highly susceptible to peer influences and pressure. Sites like Instagram, Facebook, and Snapchat provide an environment where kids are exposed to famous and normal people alike engaging in risky behaviors involving drugs and alcohol.

Celebrities such as Justin Bieber, Drake, and Cardi B consistently post pictures of themselves drinking and getting high on a variety of platforms, and that's starting to influence the young people that are viewing it.

A study conducted by the National Center on Addiction and Substance Abuse at Columbia University found that teenagers who regularly use popular social media outlets were more likely to drink, use drugs, and buy tobacco than adolescents who either did not use social media or used it less frequently. (N.p.)

These researchers found that, compared to nonusers or infrequent users of social media, this group was

- 5 times more likely to buy cigarettes
- 3 times more likely to drink
- 2 times as likely to use marijuana
- Social Media Can Contribute to Poor Mental Health
- Research has shown that there is an undeniable link between social media use, negative mental health, and low self-esteem—all of which can drive underage substance use. When teens are struggling with emotional problems, they will often turn to drugs or alcohol as a coping mechanism to help

manage their difficult feelings. Frequently checking social media platforms and comparing oneself to others can make young people feel increasingly unhappy and isolated.
- Social media not only can cause unhappiness and a general dissatisfaction with life in users but also increase the risk of developing mental health issues such as anxiety and depression. In fact, an estimated 27% of children who spend 3 or more hours a day on social media exhibit symptoms of poor mental health. Kids who are depressed or suffer from anxiety. (N.p.)

The Teen Challenge website https://www.teenchallenge.ca/get-help/canadian-drug-crisis presents an equally disturbing description recording how substance abuse increased in Canada in 2012:

- 23% of Ontario students report that they were offered, sold, or given a drug at school in the last year. That's about 219,000 students.
- 42% of Ontario students surveyed have used an illicit substance in the last year.
- 83% of Ontario students in grade 12 drink alcohol. 49% of gr. 12 students admit to binge drinking.
- In a 2008 study, 23% of 14 year-olds and 70% of 17 year-olds in Saskatchewan reported drinking 5 or more drinks within a 2-hour period at least once in the past month.
- The top four substances used by Ontario students: 58% alcohol; Cannabis (marijuana) 25%; non-prescribed use of prescription pain relievers such as codeine, Percocet, Percodan, Demerol, or Tylenol #3, 17%; Tobacco 11.7%
- 60% of illicit drug users in Canada are between the ages of 15 and 24.
- In 2005, about one Ontario student in 20 (4.4%) in grades 7 to 12 said he or she had used cocaine at least once in the past year. This is almost 43,000 students. (N.p.)

In the United States, the Centers for Disease Control and Prevention (https://www.cdc.gov/alcohol/fact-sheets/underage-drinking.htm) provided the following summary:

- Excessive drinking is responsible for more than 4,300 deaths among underage youth each year, and cost the U.S. $24 billion in economic costs in 2010.

- Although the purchase of alcohol by persons under the age of 21 is illegal, people aged 12 to 20 years drink 11% of all alcohol consumed in the United States. More than 90% of this alcohol is consumed in the form of binge drinks.
- On average, underage drinkers consume more drinks per drinking occasion than adult drinkers.
- In 2013, there were approximately 119,000 emergency room visits by persons aged 12 to 21 for injuries and other conditions linked to alcohol.
- The 2017 Youth Risk Behavior Survey found that among high school students, during the past 30 days
  - 30% drank some amount of alcohol.
  - 14% binge drank.
  - 6% drove after drinking alcohol.
  - 17% rode with a driver who had been drinking alcohol.
- In 2016, the National Survey on Drug Use and Health external icon reported that 19% of youth aged 12 to 20 years drink alcohol and 12% reported binge drinking in the past 30 days.
- In 2017, the Monitoring the Future Survey external icon reported that 8% of 8th graders and 33% of 12th graders drank during the past 30 days, and 2% of 8th graders and 19% of 12th graders binge drank during the past 30 days. (N.p.)

Gallup Poll at https://pdkpoll.org/timeline (N.p.) charts the American publics' perception of the biggest problems facing schools between 1969 and 2019. Prior to 1980, students' use of drugs was not even listed; however, in the 1980s, this issue emerged as a major concern. In each year beginning with 1986 and ending in 1992, the *percentage* of the public expressing "use of drugs" as the greatest problem was 28, 30, 32, 34, 38, 22, 22 and, in 1998, 10. At the turn of this century, the major concerns raised by the public morphed from students' use of drugs into policy issues frequently raised by teachers surrounding unionization, accountability, salaries, and funding.

Equally disturbing were student responses to drug-related questions on the "Back to School 1998 – National Survey of American Attitudes on Substance Abuse IV: Teens, Teachers and Principal" (file:///C:/Users/User/Downloads/Back-to-school-1998-national-survey-of-american-attitudes-on-substance-abuse-IV-teens-teachers-and-principals.pdf). Some of the more notable findings were:

- Teens continue to rank drugs as the single most important problem facing people their age. Teachers and principals say bad parents or family problems are the biggest problem, yet kids rank parents 10th. (p.8)
- Just 8% of 12-year-olds know a drug dealer at school; by the time they reach age 17, more than half (56%) do. (p.8)
- The social usage of marijuana is extensive. 51% of 15- to 17-year-olds have been to a party that featured pot in the last six months. 26% of 15-year-olds, 30% of 16-year-olds and 35% of 17-year-olds say a majority of the parties they have attended in the past six months had pot available. Those numbers increase to 38%, 42% and 54% for parties with alcohol. (p.8)
- A 13-year-old is almost 3 times likelier to know a teen who uses acid, cocaine, or heroin than a 12-year-old and 3 times likelier to be able to buy acid, cocaine, or heroin. (p.9)
- 27% of high school principals and 26% of high school teachers believe most students have tried pot, compared to 71% of their students. (p.10)
- Teens who smoke are 5½ times likelier to have tried marijuana, 6 times likelier to get drunk at least once a month and have drunk alcohol on 3 or more occasions in the past month, and 3 times likelier to try an illegal drug in the future than teens who don't smoke. (p.10)
- Teens who drank alcohol in the past month are 5 times likelier to smoke cigarettes, 4 times likelier to smoke marijuana, and 3 times likelier to try an illegal drug in the future. Eighty-seven percent of the students who hang out mostly with kids who drink also have friends that smoke pot. (p.10)

This report's overview stated,

> America's middle school and high school principals are living in a completely different world than their students when it comes to the existence of drug use in and around schools. If kids are to be believed, the presence of illegal drugs in schools remains widespread. But if the principals are to be believed, the war on drugs has already been won and most schools are now safe havens. Someone is dead wrong. (p.11)

By 2019, vaping emerged as the new concern. The National Institute of Drug Abuse (https://www.drugabuse.gov/news-events/news-releases/2019/12/vaping-of-marijuana-on-the-rise-among-teens) reported:

Findings from the 2019 Monitoring the Future (MTF) survey demonstrate the appeal of vaping to teens, as seen in the increased prevalence of marijuana use as well as nicotine vaping. Past year vaping of marijuana, which has more than doubled in the past two years, was reported at 20.8% among 12th graders, with 10th graders not far behind at 19.4% and eighth graders at 7.0%. Past month marijuana vaping among 12th graders nearly doubled in a single year to 14% from 7.5%—the second largest one-year jump ever tracked for any substance in the history of the survey. (The largest was from 2017-2018 with past month nicotine vaping among 12th graders). For the first time, the survey measured daily marijuana vaping, which was reported at 3.5% among 12th graders, 3.0% among 10th graders, and 0.8% among eighth graders. (N.p.)

Vaping has emerged as an alternate to the conventional intake of illicit substances thereby maintaining a worrisome trend with teenagers. The "Just Think Twice" website https://www.justthinktwice.gov/how-does-drug-use-affect-your-high-school-grades) provides a synopsis of the long-term impact on the brain:

The brain relies on chemicals called neurotransmitters to get messages from one part of the brain to the other. Each neurotransmitter attaches to its own kind of receptor—like how a key fits into a lock. This allows messages to travel through the brain on the right path. When you use drugs, it interferes with the normal traffic patterns that the neurotransmitters use. The chemical structure in the drugs can imitate and fool the receptors, lock on to them and alter the activity of the nerve cells. This "alteration" can result in messages going in the wrong direction, and reset the way your brain should act or react. . . . Teens who abuse drugs have lower grades, a higher rate of absence from school and other activities, and an increased potential for dropping out of school. . . . Students who smoke marijuana tend to get lower grades and are more likely to drop out of high school. One recent marijuana study showed that heavy marijuana use in your teen years and continued into adulthood can reduce your IQ up to as much as 8 points. (N.p.)

Another website (https://www.newbeginningsdrugrehab.org/resources/drugs-effect-on-school-performance-what-substance-abuse-is-doing-to-the-nations-youth/) produced for teens provides a synopsis of their research regarding the destructive aspect of drugs.

> The problem really started to worsen around the turn of the century when heroin and prescription drugs became more available in the nation. This was also the same time that the United States began to get really lax about marijuana too, the nation's number one gateway drug for young adults. Learning more about drugs' effects on students and school performance is a great addiction preventative measure. . . .
>
> Drugs effect focus too, making it almost impossible to study and to retain information, and students' grade averages plummet as a result. It can easily be seen that this is only the tip of the iceberg of the dwindling spiral that a teen or young adults has set himself or herself on if he or she starts abusing drugs or alcohol. . . .
>
> Declining grades, lack of interest in school subjects, lack of interest in a future career, absenteeism from school and other activities, and increased potential for dropping out of school completely are all major problems associated with adolescent substance abuse in this nation. (N.p.)

We can conclude that the quality of life for children is impacted negatively by drugs; however, they are also affected by their parents' quality of marriage. On the one hand, American society is experiencing a declining divorce rate. (Wang, 2020) With a 50-year low in 2019, the U.S. divorce rate for 1,000 married people fell from 22.6 in 1980 to 14.9 in 2019. However, the marriage rate during the same time period for 1,000 people dropped from 68.8 to 33.2. *Co-habitation and remaining single are the new norms.*

The 2016 Census Bureau (https://www.census.gov/newsroom/press-releases/2016/cb16-192.html) reported:

- The majority of America's 73.7 million children under age 18 live in families with two parents (69 percent)
- The second most common family arrangement is children living with a single mother, at 23 percent.
- Between 1960 and 2016, the percentage of children living in families with two parents decreased from 88 to 69.
- During the 1960–2016 period, the percentage of children living with only their mother nearly tripled from 8 to 23 percent and the percentage of children living with only their father increased from 1 to 4 percent. The percentage of children not living with any parent increased slightly from 3 to 4 percent. (N.p.)

The decline in the nation's family unit corresponding with the decline in religiosity is evident in this data story concerning divorce rates. In 1960, the divorce rate was 2.2 per 1,000 Americans, and reached 2.5 in 1965. By 1969, the rate jumped to 3.2 with 639,000 divorces (Olito, 2019). After the 1960s, The Pew Research Center reported that, by 2011, the share of single mothers who had never been married reached 44 percent, while half of all single mothers were divorced, separated, or widowed (Caumont, 2013). The divorce rate in 2019 was 7.6 per 1,000 Americans.

Stanton (2018) reported:

> Most recently, research conducted at Harvard's School of Public Health reveals that regularly attending church services together reduces a couple's risk of divorce by a remarkable 47 percent. Many studies, they report, have similar results ranging from 30 to 50 percent reduction in divorce risk. Happily, this holds largely true for white, black, Asian and Latino couples. (N.p.)

There remains one more tragic fact regarding America's loss of religiosity or faith. Interestingly, a Christmas television commercial by the Coca-Cola company in December 2020 portrayed a sad aspect of family life when the large delivery truck all lit up and showing Santa as the driver and reading the young child's letter, "Dear Santa, please bring dad home for Christmas." Coca-Cola understood the research and responded to a major concern in America's homes.

Livingston and Parker (2011) reported, "Just over half (55%) of men with biological children are married to the biological mother of all of those children. An additional 7% of biological fathers are cohabiting with the mother of their children." Our conclusion is that this generation is witnessing an unparalleled decline in the traditional family unit.

These aspects regarding quality of life provide credence to a message found inscribed on the American penny—IN GOD WE TRUST—and the words we sing in the well-known song, "God Bless America." The conclusion in these as well as many more iconic statements is that the nation is blessed when its people place their trust in God.

McFall (2020) buttresses this conclusion by quoting U.S. attorney general William Barr's speech regarding his belief that the American public has *misinterpreted* the actual meaning of "separation of church and state."

> "Militant secularists have long seized on that slogan as a facile justification for attempting to drive religion from the public square and to exclude religious

people from bringing a religious perspective to bear on conversations about the common good," Barr said during the virtual ceremony that had been postponed since March due to the coronavirus pandemic.

Barr said he believes that "traditional morality" has diminished, to be replaced by people who are "actively hostile" in advocating for the separation of church and state—threatening core principles in the country's democracy.

The attorney general said there is a direct correlation between the removal of religion from schools and public spaces, and the "striking increases" in urban violence, drug abuse and broken families. (N.p.)

Succinctly summarizing the situation in 2021, the family is in crisis, children are bombarded with mind- and mood-altering substances, and social unrest prevails while coping with the unsettling consequences of the COVID-19 pandemic and "Black Lives Matter."

SCHOOL VOUCHERS

Recall our points that *parents are responsible for developing their children into the kind of adults they want them to become* and that the American Constitution is *silent about education*. Unfortunately, the state still interferes with parental responsibility by inserting various controls limiting parental authority to choose.

Parents are frequently held captive in many school jurisdictions regarding which school their child can attend. School boundaries frequently limit choice and provide the only educational option available to parents. In the United States, parents are experiencing a growth in options as charter schools are undoing this limitation, and parents may still have an affordable private or independent school within reasonable distance.

Murnane et al. (2018) summarized a national trend away from private schooling:

> The share of U.S. school-age children attending private elementary schools peaked during the postwar boom of the late 1950s and early 1960s, reaching 15 percent in 1958. By the mid-1970s, it had fallen to 10 percent and remained quite steady for the rest of the 20th century. During the subsequent 15 years, it drifted downward slowly and was slightly less than 9 percent in 2015. (N.p.)

However, it is important to note that enrollments in Catholic schools dropped significantly, and these writers clarify that

> those relatively steady numbers since the mid-1970s mask significant changes in the mix of school types that make up the private-school market, driven in particular by widespread closures of Catholic schools. In 1965, 89 percent of American children who attended a private elementary school were enrolled in a Catholic school; in 2013, the comparable figure was 42 percent. By contrast, the percentage of private elementary school students who attended a non-Catholic religious school increased from 8 percent in 1965 to 40 percent in 2013. (N.p.)

In other words, Catholic schools experienced enrollment decline because of reported child abuses, while non-Catholic private school enrollments increased 400 percent during this period.

The emergence of charter schools is an equally significant trend. The webpage at https://nces.ed.gov/programs/coe/indicator_cgb.asp reports that "between fall 2000 and fall 2017, overall public charter school enrollment increased from 0.4 million to 3.1 million. During this period, the percentage of public school students who attended charter schools increased from 1 to 6 percent" (n.p.).

Parents frequently are prevented from securing an education option commensurate with their religious beliefs by the state's funding limitation. Simply stated, when the education system only funds students in a public or charter school, *parents are prisoners.* Pursuing private/independent schooling is not an option unless they have sufficient resources to enroll their child outside the publicly funded options. A Canadian school principal told a story about his secretary's husband receiving a transfer to Washington, DC, only to then refuse the opportunity because of a $25,000 private school annual tuition.

Recognizing that parents have primary responsibility while the state is obligated to provide educational options supports the notion that *funding should follow the student*—a concept frequently referred to as *voucher.* Few issues make the teachers' union's blood curdle more than providing parents a right to choose where their child will be educated. *Fear of competition underlies their arguments against choice/vouchers.*

Taxation is an element intentionally overlooked in this debate regarding education vouchers. *Parents pay taxes regardless of the school their child attends.* The union's point that funds paid to a private school means less money for public schools is a clever misrepresentation of the truth. This specious argument overlooks how the public school system has more funding available when parents select private schooling where funding does not follow their student. Simply, parents pay taxes regardless of which schooling system they choose.

Similarly, the union's argument that private schools lack accountability is also incorrect especially now that the 2015 Every Student Succeeds Act was passed by the U.S. Congress. All schools must now display their educational performance so that parents, taxpayers, and politicians can assess how well they are serving students. Every school now has greater responsibility for designing and determining educational supports and interventions.

Prothero (2017) answers a significant question:

> Have vouchers created unconstitutional entanglements between church and state since parents have used them to send their children to private religious schools? The short answer is no. In June 2002, the U.S. Supreme Court ruled that a state-enacted voucher program in Cleveland did not violate the U.S. Constitution's prohibition on government establishment of religion. In *Zelman v. Simmons-Harris*, the court found that the voucher program was constitutional because it served a valid secular purpose and it was neutral to religion—in other words, parents choose which schools the money goes to, not the state. (N.p.)

Who is responsible for a child's education is the ultimate issue? It is worthwhile repeating that parents are responsible for educating their children into the kind of adult they want their offspring to become. They, then, determine which education system should assist while fulfilling their responsibility.

THE VALUE OF ONE OF THE WORLD'S OLDEST BOOKS

Parents wanting to provide their child with an education commensurate with their wishes may also want one of the world's oldest books included as a learning resource. In addition to the teachings referenced earlier, consider the Bible's prophetical record. *When evidence demonstrates accuracy, we should permit its use in our classes of learning.* Approximately 500 prophecies are not yet fulfilled because they reach into the future and may be seen as unfolding, but Williams (2009) outlines several predictions of approximately 2000 which are now fulfilled:

Parents' Responsibility and Right

(1) Some time before 500 BC, the prophet Daniel proclaimed that Israel's long-awaited Messiah would begin his public ministry 483 years after the issuing of a decree to restore and rebuild Jerusalem (Daniel 9:25-26). He further predicted that the Messiah would be "cut off," killed, and that this event would take place prior to a second destruction of Jerusalem. Abundant documentation shows that these prophecies were perfectly fulfilled in the life (and crucifixion) of Jesus Christ. The decree regarding the restoration of Jerusalem was issued by Persia's King Artaxerxes to the Hebrew priest Ezra in 458 BC, 483 years later the ministry of Jesus Christ began in Galilee. (Remember that due to calendar changes, the date for the start of Christ's ministry is set by most historians at about AD 26. Also note that from 1 BC to AD 1 is just one year.) Jesus' crucifixion occurred only a few years later, and about four decades later, in AD 70 came the destruction of Jerusalem by Titus. (p.88)

(2) In approximately 700 BC, the prophet Micah named the tiny village of Bethlehem as the birthplace of Israel's Messiah (Micah 5:2). The fulfillment of this prophecy in the birth of Christ is one of the most widely known and widely celebrated facts in history. (p.89)

(3) In the fifth century BC, a prophet named Zechariah declared that the Messiah would be betrayed for the price of a slave—thirty pieces of silver, according to Jewish law-and also that this money would be used to buy a burial ground for Jerusalem's poor foreigners (Zechariah 11:12-13). Bible writers and secular historians both record thirty pieces of silver as the sum paid to Judas Iscariot for betraying Jesus, and they indicate that the money went to purchase a "potter's field," used—just as predicted—for the burial of poor aliens (Matthew 27:3-10). (p.89)

(4) The prophet Isaiah foretold that a conqueror named Cyrus would destroy seemingly impregnable Babylon and subdue Egypt along with most of the rest of the known world. This same man, said Isaiah, would decide to let the Jewish exiles in his territory go free without any payment of ransom (Isaiah 44:28; 45:1; and 45:13). Isaiah made this prophecy 150 years before Cyrus was born, 180 years before Cyrus performed any of these feats (and he did, eventually, perform them all), and 80 years before the Jews were taken into exile. (p.90)

Further, https://mfa.gov.il/MFA/MFAArchive/2003/Pages/The%20Land%20of%20Promise-%20The%20State%20of%20Israel.aspx, reminds us about the prophecy concerning the land of Israel preceding the modern statehood it achieved in 1948:

14 May 1948 State of Israel proclaimed:

The book of Ezekiel contains a dual prophecy to the People of Israel. In its first part, God tells the Jewish People that the land assigned to them will remain desolate as long as it is occupied by strangers, and they remain in exile. And so it was—a bleak, barren, undeveloped land—for over 2000 years. In the second half of the prophecy, God describes the signs of the incipient redemption—how the land would appear just before the Jewish People would return forever. This part of the promise, too, began to come true, during the decades preceding the establishment of the Jewish state in Eretz Israel. This is the State of Israel, referred to in a Jewish prayer as the "first flowering of our redemption." From the deep sleep of oblivion in the absence of its sons and daughters, the land finally awakened. (N.p.)

Our world's history is recorded around the birth/death of Christ (BC or Before Christ) and (anno Domini or AD) while the end of this age begins with the reconstruction of the nation of Israel in 1948. These two dates "0" and "1948" are now critical moments in human history.

It is estimated that the world's population reached one billion approximately 200 years ago and, therefore, in early Bible times, population would be measured in only millions. Many prophetical events involved small nations of people interacting with the people of Israel. However, many prophecies deal with the birth of Christ and the eventual conclusionary events of this age.

The importance of these prophecies is surpassed by the most significant message in the Bible. Knowing what has and what will happen provides us with invaluable context in our lives, but all of these messages are superseded by the most important yet simplistic of all, specifically how to experience life after death.

The absolute key to life for every student is revealed in Biblical passages such as John 3:16 where we learn that believing in God's only son, Jesus, is the basis for eternal life. All other learnings in life are secondary to this primary act of love from the God we pray to, reference on coinage, sing about and openly as well as repeatedly request His blessing. Parents, who are responsible for developing their children into the kind of adults they want them to become, *should have this option available without financial penalty.*

Earlier we referenced the overwhelming level of support parents have for some use of the Bible within the public school program, but hesitancy arises from some members in the public because of the issue regarding separation of religion and state. Providing vouchers to parents empowers them to search for the best programming for developing their *children into the kind of adults they want them to become*. Private/independent schools incorporating the *Bible as one of its textbooks* would produce significant interest and support.

Educating children from a book that has successfully predicted hundreds of circumstances and events makes history relevant. Understanding the significance and timeliness of the several hundred remaining predictions is the most important history lesson available. For example, pandemics are one of the conditions the world will face in the era when this age nears its conclusion.

A century ago, the Spanish flu killed approximately 100 million people when there were only two billion. Since AD 2000, additional pandemics occurred with SARS, Ebola, AIDS, H1N1 (Swine flu), COVID-19, and a host of lesser-known instances which have killed large populations of people. The Revelation in the Bible also predicts a futuristic cashless society which, with the advent of COVID-19, greatly accelerated this prediction. Today, our credit cards have almost completely replaced cash for fear of transmitting this dreaded virus. Swiping the card is everywhere, and "charging" limits are greatly increased.

Today, our worship of God is more contentious than ever before. While we banally continue to mouth platitudes regarding our spiritual dimension, mankind's reverence throughout North America has declined. However, interest in spiritual matters is quickly revived when a calamity overtakes our civilization.

In the USSR near the end of the last century, Premier Gorbachev's effort through Glasnost—policy or practice of more open consultative government and wider dissemination of information—and Perestroika—the policy or practice of restructuring or reforming the economic and political system—produced an amazing event. This new political climate included a desire to return Russians' interest toward Godliness.

In 1989, Russian leadership determined to influence national activity toward Christianity by securing one million Bibles from a North American publisher and gifting these to Russian soldiers. Three Russian generals flew to Vancouver, BC for a private meeting at the airport where an arrangement to have these Bibles printed in Russia was concluded. After arrangements were finalized, one of the visiting generals remarked how Premier

Gorbachev's use of Perestroika to eradicate communism was similar to what Jesus accomplished on the cross in conquering sin.

This chapter reminds us that parents are responsible for developing their child into the kind of adult they want him/her to become, and that the Bible remains one of the world's oldest and most reliable textbooks for living. Public schools are increasingly prohibited from including God's words to us and, therefore, wise parents need to search for the educational programs which will assist them in *developing their children into the kind of adults they want them to become.*

While a majority of parents support opportunities to incorporate Biblical studies, we recognize that using one of the world's oldest textbooks is not without controversy by some. Therefore, because of elements of opposition, the U.S. Supreme Court: *Stone v. Graham,* 449 U.S. 39, 42 (1980), clearly articulates that "the Bible may constitutionally be used in an appropriate study of history, civilization, ethics, comparative religion, or the like."

That life is filled with controversies and conflict is particularly evident with use of the Bible in our schools. Again, the Supreme Court—Schempp, op. cit.—declared "one's education is not complete without a study of comparative religion or the history of religion and its relationship to the advancement of civilization." A "complete education" requires an understanding of the Bible which, when denied, is every bit as controversial to parents who want it included in their child's school. Controversies imply "yes" and "no" which are resolved by managing the conditions.

Rather than choosing to deny children their complete education, legislators need to provide a funded alternative available through the voucher system *where the money follows the student.* Ultimate fairness ensures that school funding follows the student, thereby enabling parents to exercise their responsibility for educating their child toward the kind of adult they want them to be. Providing parents with a range of options, including independent schooling, ensures greater accountability for parents, while accountabilities now required in the American school system provide parents and the public with accurate and sufficiently sophisticated measurements of performance.

KEY POINTS

- Parents are responsible for educating their child into the kind of adult they want them to become.

- Governments may require parents to ensure their child be educated but *choices* remain in the parents' domain.
- During the period of high religiosity, North American schools observed many religious activities; however, most are now secularized.
- Independent school enrollment is increasing and parents want more religious observances available.
- The U.S. Supreme Court has ruled that in a *public school setting*, religious activity associated with particular religious ideology is not permitted.
- Many in the world consider the Bible as a *textbook* describing how citizens should live as well as interact with others.
- Many societal ills are rooted in our culture's disregard of Biblical teaching.
- School vouchers assist parents exercising their educational choices but are opposed by teachers' unions' fear of competition.
- American Catholic school enrollment has declined while enrollment in independent and charter schools has increased.
- The Bible, as one of the world's oldest history books, accommodates a "complete" education and is a valuable educational resource because it provides a record of history as well as prophetic descriptions of the future.
- Controversy resolved with one side winning or losing is better handled by managing the controversy and, in education, providing choice through vouchers.

Chapter 9

Democratizing Education

The previous chapter outlines a significant strategy for democratizing education by ensuring that funding is attached to the student: a reasonable expectation because *all pay taxes* directly or indirectly. This voucher system supports the parents' responsibility for raising their child into the kind of adult they want them to become. *Schools become accountable agencies when they understand that parents are gifting a child to their program and staff expertise.* While some options for this arrangement already exist, these are only a small percentage of schools and school vouchers can democratize the entire system.

Educators' ongoing lamentations about lack of parental involvement and support is no longer a justified or appropriate response. The same enthusiasm generated by a free-market approach to the distribution of goods and services could result in a new wave of commitment from parents. Another model is to declare an *open-boundary system* within each school district and then allow parents to pursue placement for their child in any school of their choosing. In other words, every school should be designated a *magnet school*.

In this *magnet school* concept, parents no longer are *assigned* a school for their child but are *drawn* to a school because of what the school is offering. Examining products for quality is a common goal within the marketplace. A similar perspective could dominate the education system if parents are able to review educational outcomes as demonstrated in chapter 3, and then use this data for determining which school is best suited to their child's educational needs. Schools provide varying levels of instructional quality and parents deserve knowing how effectively educators served their clients.

Equally important is *dispelling the myth that all schools can meet the needs of all students*. Schools, therefore, attract their clientele by majoring in programs that appeal to the strengths and interests of specific students. Such programs may revolve around the arts, components of physical education and sport, languages, subject area proficiencies leading to specific careers, special learning needs such as giftedness and learning difficulties, public speaking and presentations, technology and robotics, industry skills, social agencies, and so on. Schools could also choose to focus on a combination of programs from the foregoing list.

Naysayers to parental choice are likely to conjure up numerous "yabuts" for adopting an open-boundary system. After rejecting this concept, *because it facilitates comparison and competition between schools*, these cynics' main concern focuses on ensuring student access to their neighborhood school. Maintaining a prison mentality, where students are *confined* to a specific catchment or boundary, mitigates against the benefits of a free-market system and is a matter requiring further analysis.

Alberta's Edmonton Public Schools (EPS), with a student population of approximately 100,000, implemented school-based decision making with schools controlling all aspects of their budgets. This decentralization quickly morphed into control of a school's mission beyond core education requirements. Parents living within a school's catchment retained first right of entry leaving the remaining student spaces to parents from other parts of the school district. Our regional studies determined that only 48 percent of students attended their neighborhood's magnet school.

Many parents exercised an option to have their child attend a different school basing their decision on issues such as the school's mission, academic record, special programming and services, proximity of a school to the parent's workplace, and so on. We examined the academic success demonstrated by students in this school district with *consistently improving test scores as they proceeded through the grades*.

Providing parents with the responsibility to select their child's school also motivates them to make certain that their choice is vindicated. Their dream of aligning their child's interest and talent with a specific school's mission inspires their own interest in the goals of the school and how well it is achieving. EPS' success in achieving higher levels of academic success as students progress through the grades may have several contributing factors and school choice must be included in the list.

Per pupil funding is an issue when parents choose to enroll their children in different schools; however, the concern is readily resolved when all schools are within the same organizational structure or district. At the beginning of the school year, the funding allocated to each student follows that student to the appropriate school. Some school districts go a step further and make allowance for students changing schools during the term and apply a midterm adjustment. *The critical principle is that money follows a student to their selected school.*

COMPARING MAGNET, CHARTER, AND PRIVATE SCHOOLS

Magnet schools are somewhat similar to charter schools with a few noteworthy differences. Charter schools are K–12 institutions, funded with taxpayer money *but managed privately*. They are semi-autonomous operating under a written contract with a state, district, or entity (referred to as an authorizer or sponsor). This contract—or charter—details how the school will be organized and managed, what students will be expected to achieve, and how success will be measured. Many charters are exempt from a variety of laws and regulations affecting other public schools if they continue to meet the terms of their charters.

These charter provisions incorporate higher levels of accountability, but their exemption from laws and regulations constraining other public schools has special appeal. While visiting one charter school along the California border with Mexico, which was also designated as America's top school, the principal provided significant insight into the school's lofty standing. In his opinion, a provision placing all staff on *one-year contracts* was the critical variable. Nonrenewal of a contract even jeopardized ongoing employment within the school district.

Magnet schools, on the other hand, are not semi-autonomous but totally accountable to the local school board while operating within the jurisdiction's regulatory and contractual obligations. Rather than reporting to a semi-autonomous board, they work with a Parent Advisory Council (PAC). School administrators are obligated to *consult* with the PAC on matters such as the school mandate, education plan including staff organization, student discipline policy, and other general matters. Another significant discussion activity involving the PAC follows the annual accumulation of results contained within the school's report card described earlier.

Sponsors, another critical component of charter schools, are not a requirement but a recommendation for magnet schools. Several partnerships can be identified which support the school's mission statement and provide opportunities for students to engage with the business community. Unlike sponsors, partnerships with magnet schools can be many and in competition with each other, and they can also change from year to year.

Private or independent schools are a more dramatic approach for accommodating parent choice; however, they provide educational opportunities, such as religious instruction, for students. The private school model frequently serves a community where many public schools are available. Registration into these private schools usually involves liningup on registration day using a first-come-first-served model. Once a child is in school, other family members receive preferential treatment.

A provision for ensuring that families are not separated should also be applied to magnet schools. In some respects, this commitment is antithetical to the magnet concept because children in a family usually are different; however, parents may feel more comfortable knowing that family members are together. The choice to separate or be clannish is another element of parental choice.

Public funding for private schools is a contentious issue with many educators voicing concern about their competition receiving financial support. In Canada, funding from provincial governments varies and is usually confined to a portion of the school's operating expenses. Private school operators are responsible for generating funds for capital expenditures.

TEACHERS' UNIONS

Centuries ago, North America was the last "New World." Many people left Europe to begin a new life where they would be free to pursue their dreams. Some were able to venture across the ocean with considerable financial wealth, which they could use to begin a life while dealing with the many hardships of their new world. Many others fled from harassment and persecution in their European locations with nothing more than a few clothes and memorabilia. North America promised people a fresh start without the social and economic constraints of the old order in Europe.

Those pursuing this dream included some who held on to conventions designed to exert control over workers. Their intent was to organize laborers into groups and then act as their representatives. This kind of activity, in its *best expression*, can be an act of heroic altruism because many people find it difficult to represent themselves when dealing with an employer.

More typically, however, those who led did so with a desire for power analogous to the "bosses" and owners whom they despised. Rather than serving their colleagues, they became tyrannical in disregarding dissenting opinions and in forcing all to participate in their enterprise. There are many instances in these organizations where leadership was corrupt to the extent of being criminal.

On the other side of the coin, history is replete with examples of how workers were disadvantaged by greedy employers. They needed to be rescued by organizations committed to assisting them in their plight. There is a range in people's capacity to stand up for themselves when confronted with unfair management practices. Governments who become aware of unscrupulous management have a responsibility to set standards and enact protective legislation. There is also a time and place for organizations *who are fully accountable to the people they seek to serve* and to the public welfare to provide protection and support for un-empowered people.

Teacher unions are controversial in educational politics. The controversy generated is whether they are a *stumbling block* to reform or *advocates* for better schools and better teachers. Public attitudes regarding this differing perspective are shifting. Peterson et al. (2012) asked Americans about whether teacher unions have a generally positive or negative effect on schools.

While 41 percent of the public selected the neutral position, those with a positive view of unions dropped to 22 percent in 2012 from 29 percent in 2011. The survey's most striking finding was that 58 percent of teachers took a positive view of unions in 2011, and only 43 percent did in 2012. The number of teachers holding negative views of unions nearly doubled to 32 percent from 17 percent. Generally, individual teachers had little control over their union dues when these are diverted for political use.

On June 27, 2018, the U.S. Supreme Court recognized the right of public employees to choose whether to financially support their union based upon the freedom of speech protected by the First Amendment of the U.S. Constitution. The *Janus v. AFSCME* ruling for all teachers and other public employees who like their unions and wish to maintain their membership in them while nonetheless allowing those who believe that their unions do not meet their personal needs to stop paying compulsory fees to their unions. The website, https://ra.nea.org/wp-content/uploads/2018/06/Janus-Explainer.pdf, provides additional explanation:

> Under the decision, no state or school district or other public employer anywhere in the country can permit a union to charge non-members a fee for the costs of their representation. Such fees—often called fair share or agency fees—had previously been permitted in many states with public sector collective bargaining and allowed unions who represented a bargaining unit to spread the costs of representing that unit in bargaining across all employees in the unit. The Janus decision means that unions in the public sector can no longer charge nonmembers fair share or agency fees. NEA and its affiliates who previously did collect such fees have now stopped doing so in order to comply with the decision. (p.1)

Accessing information about the political use of union dues in Canada demonstrates a significant lack of transparency. Stinson (2014) provides a succinct and telling summary about the unions' abilities to influence political processes in Canada in comparison to other democracies:

> Canada is unique among major Western economies in allowing both the collection of mandatory union dues and the use of that money to fund political activities. . . . In the United Kingdom, workers cannot be compelled to join a union as a condition of employment; they can opt in or out.
>
> France, Germany and Italy prohibit the use of compulsory union dues for political contributions. And in Australia, workers can neither be forced to join a union if one exists at their place of work nor have to pay the portion of union dues that would go toward political activities. Meanwhile, those countries all have systems in place that require unions to disclose basic financial information about major expenses.
>
> In Canada, union financials are utterly opaque. According to the Ministry of Finance, about $860-million worth of union dues were deducted from tax returns in 2012, the last year for which numbers are available, up from $705-million in 2007. There are estimates that the total amount of dues collected runs into the billions. That money, which is exempt from federal taxes, can be spent however

the union chooses: office space, staff salaries, organized protests, political attack ads. And the employee has no say over any of it. (N.p.)

Many Canadian teachers' unions lack accountability, especially regarding their involvement and influence in political activities. Most important, closed shop unions operate with the lowest level of accountabilities. Members have no choice but to yield to the union hierarchy's decisions; however, the remedy in this issue can be achieved if teachers could *democratically choose association*.

Closed Shop

This section's focus is about democratizing education including how teachers in the education system have been *required* to give up their individual freedom in order to work. It is not a section focusing on the merits of unions, which are organizational forces today for good and bad, and sometimes simultaneously both. Rather, it is a section about the malevolent influence of a union practice known as closed shop—that practice which requires employees to remain members of the union at all times in order to remain employed.

The *closed shop* arrangement is anti-democratic because employees are forced into an arrangement from which they cannot escape unless they are willing to leave their employment. They are not free to make personal agreements with their employer *even when that employer would want to reward exceptional service*. One superintendent spoke of his region's intention to provide teachers with a bonus based on their outstanding work. The initiative was quickly scuttled because it had not been sanctioned by the union office and was forbidden by a collective agreement stipulating that all teachers were to be paid according to the contract. It did not allow individualized monetary recognition.

Closed shop also creates confusion for the employee. We easily understand how employees are responsible to their employers, but *it is puzzling to many employees that they also work for the union*. For example, employees who refuse to fulfill a union requirement such as picketing can have their union card canceled, which means they would no longer qualify to work with that employer. Ultimately, closed shop arrangements provide union leadership with significant power over their membership.

North Americans benefit from their governments' adherence to principles of freedom. It seems incongruous, then, that organizations are permitted which limit peoples' freedom to choose. In essence, a closed shop arrangement is similar to citizens' experiences in countries governed by one political party—for example, China. Allowing people to make choices in areas such as government, religion, *and work should be everyone's democratic right*.

Right-to-Teach Legislation

Across the English-speaking world, notable differences in legislation exist in regard to the right-to-teach environment. An issue in such an environment pertains to whether teachers have the right to work *without a membership component*. Another issue relates to whether or not a teacher has the right to formally *opt out of the union* while retaining the right to teach. While there are many issues involved, these two get at the heart of whether countries, states, and provinces operate a closed shop.

In Australia, New Zealand, and Great Britain, union membership is *not* required, dues are *not* required, and there are separate organizations dealing with collective bargaining and professional activity. This separation in focus is significant because teachers can pursue their professional development interests without becoming embroiled in issues related to union politics.

The Canadian situation varies from having a province with the most "closed" environment in the English-speaking world to provinces and territories where union membership is optional, dues are not required from nonmembers, and there is only one organization identified to represent teachers choosing to become members. For example, Alberta law requires that all public school teachers be a member of a specific union that conducts activities associated with both negotiations and professionalism. This model demonstrates the most extreme closed shop because government decrees that a public school teacher must join.

On the other end of the spectrum Prince Edward Island makes union membership optional (teachers must opt out in writing) and dues are not required from nonmembers. The only opting-in option is to the one organization that exists. This model increases accountability for the union beyond that which is evident in Alberta because teachers can *choose* whether they will join.

Attempts at Curbing Unionism

An issue in this discussion pertains to who determines right to work. Is it a legislated decision made by the state, as is the case in Alberta, or by an employer such as a school board? For many decades, British Columbia's (B.C.) legislation was similar to Alberta's where teachers were required to be a union member in order to teach in a public school. In the late 1980s, B.C. withdrew this requirement but did not enact legislation forbidding employers to make union membership a requirement, as have many American states.

The teachers' union in B.C. effectively mobilized their locals and, after several strikes on this issue, was able to insert language into every public-school employer's collective agreement that employment as a teacher in the district required membership in the union. In some instances, teachers already employed were "grandfathered" out of the union until such time as they left that district. The provincial government resolved a contentious political issue about the morality of forcing teachers into a union by offloading the issue to local school districts. *Now local school boards are the ones responsible for denying teachers a basic human freedom.*

The National Labor Relations Board website—https://www.nlrb.gov/about-nlrb/who-we-are/our-history/1947-taft-hartley-substantive-provisions—describes how the United States attempted to curb rising unionism by passing the Taft–Hartley Act in 1947 enacted that

> employees had the right to refrain from participating in union or mutual aid activities except that they could be required to become members in a union as a condition of employment. . . . [It also] declared "the closed shop illegal, but provided that employers could sign a union shop agreement under which employees could be required to join the union on or after the 30th day of employment." (N.p.)

This legislation was directed at demobilizing the labor movement by limiting their ability to strike.

Power and Weakness

In 2013, the Canadian government also considered curbing the powers of organized labor. Black (2013) responded to a teachers' strike in Ontario and succinctly described how unionization progressed successfully into the public sector.

For many years, the often explicit understanding was that public employees would be less well-paid than those in the private sector, but would have greater job security and, in general, less challenging employment. The unionization of the public service consigned that rule of thumb to the proverbial dust-bin of history, and public-service unions began leading organized labour in militancy, while feasting on the weakness and cowardice of political employers. (N.p.)

A recent Canadian study (Lammam et al. 2015) reported that public sector employees at the federal level earn 17 percent more than comparable workers in the private sector and, if benefits are included, cost 42 percent more. At the provincial (B.C.) level, the advantage is 8 percent and 25 percent, respectively, while at the municipal level the advantage averaged 11 percent and 36 percent, respectively. Black's thesis is that public sector unions win "big" because they are "feasting on the weakness and cowardice of political employers." Not only have they retained greater job security but they also have reversed the pay paradigm.

Regarding the teacher strike in Ontario, Black went on to say,

It is now a familiar three-hanky tear-jerker to see teachers' union representatives passionately explaining that the last thing they wish to do by striking in the middle of the school year is hold the students hostage or impinge on the money-earning capacity of their parents; but that is, of course, what they are doing and why they are doing it. (N.p.)

Without doubt, teacher unions enjoy a record of success in the U.S. as well. At his retirement speech in 2009, former general counsel for the National Educators' Association, Bob Chanin said,

I have found it increasingly necessary to spend time defending NEA and its affiliates against attacks from government agencies, conservative and right-wing groups, and unfriendly media. Why you may ask is this so? Why are these conservative and right-wing bastards picking on NEA and its affiliates? I will tell you why. It is the price we pay for success. NEA and its affiliates have been singled out because they are the most effective union in the United States. . . . It is not because we care about children. And it is not because we have a vision of a great public school for every child. NEA and its affiliates are effective advocates because we have power. And we have power because there are more than

3.2 million people who are willing to pay us hundreds of millions of dollars in dues each year. (McCluskey 2009; N.p.)

When we link Chanin and Black's arguments together, we hit the proverbial "nail on the head." When *power* confronts *weakness and cowardice,* there is a clear winner in a negotiating contest that is all about winning and losing. A central theme in this book is that politicians, who manage their public sector, are unable to handle the power of their unionized employees. The power is in the voting booth when there are so many people employed in the public sector. Weakness and cowardice arise from the reality that the next election is never far away.

For this reason, governments do their best to negotiate agreements that will expire after the next election and, preferably, in the year after the election. A strike just prior to an election places government members at a disadvantage unless they want to make labor negotiations the central issue. Labor unrest in the year following an election is deemed to be acceptable, if necessary, because there is usually sufficient time to heal the rift between the union and the politicians before the next election.

The union's power is enhanced by the closed shop provision. *Absence of choice absents accountability.* Union leadership can push the boundaries of their thirst for power; yet, they remain immune from the accountability for improving student outcomes. Their bottom-line mandate of "less work with more pay" for their members does not enhance service to the school system's clients. Their quenchless thirst for power achieved without concomitant accountability while reducing management's capacity to operate an efficient and effective school system has produced a more toxic environment.

Accountability in public sector organizations such as education must undergo greater examination. In complex relationships such as is evident in our school system, different types of accountability are involved: some bodies provide funding while others administer it and set policies. When dual accountabilities are evident, the primary accountability is usually to the organization that provides the most funding.

Accordingly, in our North American school systems, three political bodies are accountable in varying degrees. In the United States, the federal government provides a minor portion of the funding whereas, in Canada, funding from the national government is nonexistent. In both of these countries, the state or province is the significant funding source which may be accompanied by taxation powers within the school district. To varying degrees then, politicians are assigned accountability for the quality of services provided in improving student outcomes.

Union leadership does not fit into this accountability paradigm because they do not fund education and there is no provision for the public to vote them out of office if there is dis-satisfaction with the quality of service. Instead, union leadership is immune to accountability and their power and success in limiting the authority of educational managers to improve the system is one of our foci. Without attaching accountability for improving student success to teacher unions, there is a gap in democratic accountability and our education system is at risk.

This description is not a criticism of teacher unions at the theoretic level: they are merely fulfilling their responsibilities and functioning in accordance with their mandate. Their success is well documented! Rather, the concern is focused on what has become an inappropriate relationship where a lack of accountability is too evident. Black's description of weak and cowardly politicians requires a new paradigm because we now live in a global community.

The union's phenomenal success should be a wake-up call for a new accountability structure to be implemented that includes union leadership. In the United States, for example, student achievement is being incorporated into staff evaluations which will be linked with their pay. Linking performance and pay is a revolutionary practice in education, and a similarly transformational re-shaping of union politics is conceivable by attaching union leadership's pay to student success. Their success at the bargaining table in achieving status as co-managers of the school system requires that their leadership be held accountable for student success and other outcomes determined and overseen by the public.

Unions are an adversarial special interest group seeking to improve the fortunes of their members; yet, they ardently want to be considered as educational partners. A partnership with government—which leads and allocates funds—and with parents—who are the system's clients—and the public—who pays the bills—is conceivable. Partners share in the good and the bad. In this partnership, consequences are applied based on performance recorded on the school system's report card.

There is a second component to this partnership. Just as political leadership should be removed when system results are not improving, a similar consequence should be applied to the partners providing leadership to the service providers. Just as political leadership can be "punted" when the school system fails to deliver quality educational services, so should the partner's leadership be removed. In this manner, a shared vision replaces the selfishness that currently exists. Trust between the partners increases because the accountability is equalized.

The education system requires transformation in many areas including its relationship with the teachers' union. The emphasis should focus on introducing accountability for the union's hierarchy by eliminating closed shop and incorporating student achievement into the union's mandate. A closed shop union in one region can impact many other regions where such an arrangement does not exist. A union practice known as whipsawing has the capacity then to transfer contractual provisions from one district to another even when a district is non-union.

KEY POINTS

- Magnet schools are another example of democratizing a school system.
- EPS have a three-decade experience with magnet schools.
- Charter schools are privately run and operate without union controls.
- Magnet schools operate under the rules of a local school board.
- Centuries ago, North America offered a "new world"; however, some came with a desire to incorporate "old world" ideology such as unionization.
- The U.S. Supreme Court's Janus decision means that unions in the public sector can no longer charge nonmembers fair share or agency fees.
- Closed shop places teachers within the control of the union.
- Governments attempt to limit union power with right-to-work legislation.
- Teachers' unions operate in the public sector with significant political power.
- Requiring greater accountability for union leadership is achievable by attaching these to the accountabilities of the system report card outlined in chapter 3.

Chapter 10

Schools Deal with the Sexual Revolution

North American society is consumed with sexuality issues since the turn of this century, and sex education went well beyond a study of the major parts of the body. This century's focus changed from viewing heterosexuality as the only acceptable expression of sexuality to changing homosexuality from deviant to acceptable. Four American states—California, Colorado, New Jersey, and Illinois—now require that the history of lesbian, gay, bisexual, and transgender be included in their curriculum. This chapter is focused specifically on how the transgender issue affects our schools.

Walsh (2019) reported on U.S. Supreme Court deliberations:

> "[The] big issue right now raging the country is bathroom usage—same-sex bathroom usage," Justice Sonia Sotomayor said during the arguments.
>
> It went without saying that that issue is raging most fiercely in public schools, where there have been numerous skirmishes in recent years about transgender students using facilities that align with their gender identities.
>
> "Let me move beyond the bathroom to another example," Justice Samuel A. Alito Jr. said later. "And it is not before us, but it will be coming. So a transgender woman is not permitted to compete on a woman's college sports team. Is that discrimination on the basis of sex in violation of Title IX?" (N.p.)

In Canada, British Columbia now provides ready-to-use, grade-appropriate SOGI-inclusive lesson plans that align with this curriculum. Teachers can adapt or adopt SOGI 1 2 3 lesson plans to meet the needs of their classrooms. Its message is:

> Sexual orientation and gender identity (SOGI) is not its own curriculum; it is one aspect of diversity that is embedded across a range of grades and subject areas. SOGI-inclusive education is fundamentally about learning to treat each other with dignity and respect regardless of our differences. All students need to see themselves and their families reflected in lessons, language and practices. Like other forms of inclusion in schools, the goal of SOGI-inclusive education is for everyone to understand the diverse society that we live in and to feel safe, valued, and respected. (https://bc.sogieducation.org/sogi3) (N.p.)

Transgenderism and a number of other sexual preferences, options, and practices are the current points of discussion in the ongoing dialog with social conservatives and progressives. Across millennia, the definition of gender was biological: Did the baby have a penis or a vagina, an X or a Y chromosome? Transgenderism shifts the focus from the physical and the biological to the social and psychological and is described as follows:

> Gender identity is a person's sense of their gender. They can be a woman, man, combination of these, or something else. Some people feel like no gender identity fits for them, and that's ok too. Somebody's identity can change. As time goes by, how much or little someone identifies with man-ness, woman-ness, and as other genders can change. . . . Many trans people may know early on that they don't fit with the gender that people think they are. Some people find out later in their lives or take longer to know for sure. Either way, they also might not feel comfortable telling people they love (http://sexted.org/faq/gender-identity-transgender/?gclid=EAIaIQobChMI95es5e2Q6QIVA6SzCh1YhAXZEAAYASAAEgKgYvD_BwE (n.p.).

Washrooms were traditionally male *or* female but not male *and* female. The Starbucks coffee chain can accommodate a multi-gender need because their washrooms are designed for one person and the door can just be labeled "washroom." School washrooms accommodate groups of students as do change rooms for sports activities, and accommodating transgender students provides a conundrum for schools.

Some people are surprised and upset that this issue has caused parents to flee the public school system. The earlier matter, related to study of the difference in body parts, was bothersome to many parents because this was occurring with children in early grades. However, when various societal groups then used the court system and pressured governments to delve into areas related to values, many parents chose to leave their public school system for private or homeschooling. Life experiences and sincerely held religious beliefs led many in public to lose trust in a school system that no longer accommodated, let alone affirmed, their perspective.

In 2020, transgenderism in sports became a central issue facing the school system as boys identifying as girls replaced girls on the winner's podiums. Stanescu (2020) reported that Idaho enacted a law to protect female athletes from being dethroned by students with male body parts, whereas at least seventeen states recognized biological boys participating in female sports.

The historical guidelines for sports were outlined in a document located at https://www.womenssportsfoundation.org/wp-content/uploads/2016/11/issues-related-to-girls-and-boys-competing-with-and-against-each-other-in-sports-and-physical-activity-settings-the-foundation-position.pdf., with related stated preferences as follows:

- Prior to puberty, there is no gender-based physiological reason to separate females and males in sports competition.
- Coeducational competition, when appropriately governed to prevent female or male advantage, is desirable.
- Voluntary, single-sex team for girls is the only permissible instance of sex segregation in athletics.
- When a school does not offer a team for girls in a certain sport, a school must allow the girl to try out to participate on the boys' team when girls are underrepresented among a school's athletes and possess the interest and ability to participate.
- Boys should be allowed to play on a girls' team only when there is no team for boys offered in that sport, boys are underrepresented with regard to total athletic opportunities, and the strength and skill levels of the boys are comparable to those of the girls
- Boys cannot participate on girls' teams when there is no team offered for boys in the sport if girls are underrepresented in the sports program. While courts have found girls have the right to compete on boys' teams under the EPC and Title IX, the courts have not granted boys the same access to girls' teams. (N.p.)

In 2021, the national political scene intervened with a directive from newly elected president, Joe Biden. Schrier (2021) reported:

> Amid Inauguration Day talk of shattered glass ceilings, on Wednesday President Biden delivered a body blow to the rights of women and girls: the Executive Order on Preventing and Combating Discrimination on the Basis of Gender Identity or Sexual Orientation. On day one, Mr. Biden placed all girls' sports and women's safe spaces in the crosshairs of the administrative state.
>
> The order declares: "Children should be able to learn without worrying about whether they will be denied access to the rest room, the locker room, or school sports. . . . All persons should receive equal treatment under the law, no matter their gender identity or sexual orientation." The order purports to direct administrative agencies to begin promulgating regulations that would enforce the Supreme Court's 2020 decision *Bostock v. Clayton County*. In fact, it goes much further.
>
> In *Bostock*, the justices held that Title VII of the Civil Rights Act of 1964 prohibited an employer from firing an employee on the basis of homosexuality or "transgender status." Justice Neil Gorsuch, writing for a 6-3 majority, took pains to clarify that the decision was limited to employment and had no bearing on "sex-segregated bathrooms, locker rooms, and dress codes"—all regulated under Title IX of the 1972 Education Amendments. "Under Title VII, too," the majority added, "we do not purport to address bathrooms, locker rooms, or anything else of the kind."
>
> The Biden executive order is far more ambitious. Any school that receives federal funding—including nearly every public high school—must either allow biological boys who self-identify as girls onto girls' sports teams or face administrative action from the Education Department. (N.p.)

A negative response in some parts of the United States was immediate, and Srikanth (2021) reported that Montana, for example, introduced a bill that would require:

> Public school athletic teams to be designated based on biological sex, effectively preventing transgender students from participating in gendered sports. The bill cites "inherent differences between men and women," including testosterone levels, which are already regulated by ruling bodies such as the NCAA.

The association requires one year of hormone treatment as a condition prior to competing on a female team.

"I submit to you that, if you don't pass legislation such as this, that it will come to the day where there will be no room, no place, for women to compete, and at that point, I say to you, where shall we go, against whom shall we compete, and to whom shall we turn for redress?" said Idaho Republican state Rep. Barbara Ehardt, who sponsored a similar bill in her state that has been challenged in court and issued a temporary injunction. (N.p.)

Tausz (2021) with the *New York Post* responded to the new directive indicating that

a recent study suggests that male-to-female trans athletes retain physical advantages over their female peers even after a year of testosterone suppression. Fairness aside, this is dangerous. . . . By explicitly including "children," Biden signals to American girls that he accepts gender ideology's view that *embodied* femininity means nothing. Today, trans ideology is influencing record numbers of girls and teens to despise their female bodies and do irreparable injury to their fertility and health. Biden's order shrugs at their fate. (N.p.)

High school sports are known to be extremely competitive to the degree that coaches win or lose their livelihood. Will they now bolster their careers by actively recruiting transgender students and excluding females from school teams? Many American star athletes are now voicing their concern that females will be excluded from achieving their athletic aspirations.

KEY POINTS

- Transgenderism is the most recent sexuality issue facing schools.
- Transgenderism shifts the focus from the physical and the biological to the social and psychological.
- Prior to this issue, when schools did not offer a team for one gender, that gender may participate on the other gender's team.
- Newly elected President Biden changed the issue when he signed an executive order permitting transgender boys to play on girl's teams.
- This issue of permitting males on female teams is facing strong opposition.

Chapter 11

Students' Cell Phones

The rapid advent of technology has changed school life, and cell phones are an example of a more pernicious incursion of technology entering the school system. A majority of parents likely support equipping their child with a means for easy contact; however, this communication device is providing additional challenges for educators. Statewide policies appear to be lacking thereby delegating decisions to the local school regarding students' cell phone access: a delegation of authority frequently implying confusion regarding advantages.

Akers (quoted in Turnitin, "Letter to Your Principal: Cell Phones," n.p.) reviewed school-level policies in one state (Kentucky) and summarized these as either prohibiting student access during the school day or permitting access while in the "off" position. Parents generally support equipping their child with a cell phone as a means for immediate warning of a school intruder. Their concern stems from the spate of school shootings in recent decades.

According to Akers' interviews with principals, their concerns are listed as follows:

1. Bullying or harassing other students with unwanted voice or text messages.
2. Text messaging or phoning friends during class time.
3. Cheating (i.e., recording, sending or receiving test questions and/or answers).

4. Secretly taking inappropriate photographs of other students and distributing them.
5. Photographing exam answers to use during the exam.
6. Phoning in bomb threats to the school, which cannot always be traced.
7. Phoning others outside the school to meet at the school during or after school to witness or participate in a fight or confrontation.
8. Experts have stated that cell phones could be used to detonate a bomb if it is near or on the school's campus.
9. In a true emergency, massive cell phone usage can overload cellular phone systems, crippling critical official and emergency communication.
10. In larger school districts, gang members have, reportedly, used cell phones to communicate with one another during school hours.
11. School administrators and law enforcement officials have learned that drug deals have been made via cell phones during school hours.
12. During school emergencies, massive numbers of students have called their parents via cell phones, and, as a result, those parents have bombarded the campuses, thwarting emergency protocols and procedures. (N.p.)

Akers summative assessment of the current predicament is that "the current barrage of illegal and immoral acts committed daily (on cell phones by students during the school day) far outweigh the parent's right to talk (and in some cases, interfere) with their children during a school emergency" (n.p.).

The New York Times (https://www.nytimes.com/2020/02/06/learning/what-students-are-saying-about-how-much-they-use-their-phones-and-whether-we-should-be-worried.html) on February 6, 2020, reviewed this issue of students' cell phones and summarized their conclusion:

> Some students admitted to spending upward of eight hours a day online, with the majority averaging around two to four hours. Some said their devices were a reasonable escape from the pressures of teenage life, while others explained they were essential for school. And still others raised an insightful question: Why is their "phone addiction" perceived as more harmful than that of the adults in their lives? (N.p.)

Yes, children see parents' addiction to their cell phone and follow suit with their own. At the same time, proponents might argue that students learn proper usage by ignoring their phones when engaged in their classrooms, just like their parents are expected when engaged in their work activities and the phone interrupts conversations.

Therefore, a policy that might address responsible use of cell phones for students is to permit phones in the "off" position while stored in their backpacks. Providing exceptions to this policy invokes confusion about the rule. School staff can release students to call for emergency services when such a circumstance occurs. However, if the phone is used during school time for a non-emergency, it is confiscated and returned later according to prescribed times outlined in the school's policy handbook.

KEY POINTS

- Parents generally support equipping their child with a cell phone as a means for immediately warning of a school intruder.
- School administrators are concerned with students' immoral and illegal uses of their cell phones.
- Permitting cell phones in the "off" position while carried in the student's backpack for emergency availability appears to be the most appropriate compromise.

Chapter 12

Unfairness of Prolonged Summer Vacations

Our nations' schools broadly incorporate two organizational practices deleterious to our children's academic achievement. In a culture where achieving change is difficult, educators hold onto these practices despite evidence suggesting that they inhibit many students from achieving their potential. An earlier chapter discussed the educational issues of the relative-age-effect and how too many students are disadvantaged by a lengthy registration window. This chapter examines why the educational system must reconsider how schools organize time for learning to overcome an educational handicap created by summer loss.

THE CHAOS OF SUMMER VACATION

This chapter questions the efficacy of providing students with long periods of vacation, which introduces the concept of *forgetting rates*. We know that students learn at different rates, and significant professional development is undertaken to personalize student learning to accommodate these varying rates of learning. What we leave out of our reform effort is that students also forget at varying rates, and *we dismiss the amount of time wasted while attempting to recover what is forgotten.*

As usual, there is personal bias that blocks this issue from receiving greater attention. Education's workforce benefits from a phenomenal perk with an approximately ten weeklong, prime-time vacation. Some educators use this time to upgrade their skills or seek additional employment, but, for the majority, summer days are filled with family and outdoor activities. "This is the life" and "it doesn't get better than this" are two phrases that might describe what exhilarated educators experience the day after school is over for another year.

Dame Edith Wharton (https://www.newtownbee.com/07082002/summer-afternoon-summer-afternoon-to-me-those-have-always-been-the-two-mo/) described this period of the year as, "summer afternoon—summer afternoon: to me those have always been the two most beautiful words in the English language."

Hal Borland (https://www.brainyquote.com/quotes/hal_borland_390186) summarized how many of us rationalize the seasons with the words, "summer is a promissory note signed in June, its long days spent and gone before you know it, and due to be repaid next January." These words describe how most of us view summer and why being free from work responsibilities is a significant employment perk. Anyone tampering with continuation of this perk does so at their own peril.

However, we are a global village and technology is making us increasingly so. Countries all over the world are intent on providing their citizens with a North American high standard of living. Accomplishing such massive improvement requires them to undercut our costs and be more efficient. They want to have a more educated workforce than ours because *learning well is related to living well*. While the world's overall standard of living is always improving, the economic system is based on winners and losers. We know this to be true because even within the same country, there are regions which go through prolonged periods of economic suffering relative to other regions.

We can see long-term effects in two examples. Japanese cars in the 1970s were of such poor quality that we referred to them as a "rust bucket of bolts." In recent years, the superior quality of these Japanese cars has enabled them to capture a significant share of the global market. Perhaps even more astonishingly, a quality North American-produced golf shirt cost more than $100 in 2000. Today, golf shirts of a similar quality produced in Southeast Asia and shipped to North America can be purchased for one-half the price despite many years of inflation.

The impact in North America is keenly felt in certain sectors of the economy as manufacturing jobs have disappeared. The point is that the marketplace is much more competitive as quality rises and costs hold steady or decrease and companies everywhere scramble to remain relevant.

Silicon Valley, a key world center for technology, reports (https://www.mercurynews.com/2018/01/17/h-1b-foreign-citizens-make-up-nearly-three-quarters-of-silicon-valley-tech-workforce-report-says/) that "About 71 percent of tech employees in the Valley are foreign born, compared to around 50 percent in the San Francisco-Oakland-Hayward region, according to a new report based on 2016 census data" (n.p.).

If we believe that a well-educated citizenry is essential for future economic success, then we must be prepared to reexamine our presuppositions and embrace invigorating change. In the world of education, this may mean that our tradition of providing students with approximately 1,000 hours of formal schooling in a given year may be found to be insufficient, especially when our "competitors" in Asia provide their children with almost ten additional *workweeks* per year.

We can readily improve achievement but we don't. Our problem is not a lack of understanding, *but a lack of will*. For example, we know what needs to be done and could be done to improve student achievement, but we prefer clinging to past conventions in the mistaken belief that preservation of the status quo is to be preferred to the irritations associated with change.

The complexity of the educational problem associated with a prolonged summer vacation is confounded by the instructional time wasted preparing to shut down the school for summer break. During this winding-down period, inventories are taken of school materials, such as library books, which necessitate nonuse of these resources. Classroom labs are closed to check supplies and to ascertain that all will be in order for the new term. Added to this is the time consumed in a general school-wide cleanup: bulletin boards need to be stripped of student work and teacher resources need to be packed up and stored.

More importantly, to compound the problem, teachers at this time of the year are feeling so exhausted and pressured by year-end activities that they lower their expectations for student effort. Year-end parties with additional outdoor play activities like field trips are normal, and at the end of the day teachers look to exit the school as quickly as possible. For several weeks, time is spent on activities of dubious value and no particular relationship to the curriculum. Finally, when the year is over, there is a collective sigh of relief even though it is recognized that there has been little real learning, as defined by the curriculum, during the wind-down segment of the year.

The year-end loss of focus mirrors the problems experienced at the beginning of the next school term. All the supplies and resources the teachers packed during the final days of the school year they must now unpack. Students must once again be re-educated to observe the behavioral routines adults expect of them. Without this, it is impossible to develop a learning culture, and without a learning culture, students will be unable to focus on the task of learning.

Students new to the school must be welcomed and oriented in such a way that they integrate successfully into the community of learners. This occurs at a time when teachers and administrators are busy addressing a host of administrative duties which are an integral part of a new schooling year.

But these challenges pale in comparison to the biggest challenge of all: *teachers must help students relearn all that was forgotten in the long summer interlude.* Much of the first month of the new school year in elementary classrooms is spent reviewing mathematics and language arts skills. Repeated annually over the course of several years, these reviews constitute many months of wasted time merely caused by the long summer break which our forefathers instituted to facilitate the family's farming activities.

THE IMPACT OF SOCIOECONOMIC STATUS ON STUDENT LEARNING

A significant question pertains to whether learning loss is universal? In other words, are there categories of students who are disadvantaged to a greater degree by having these long breaks from formal learning? If there is a pattern that can predict which students are disadvantaged, the school system is then operating in an unfair manner if action is not taken to ameliorate their situation. We must come to terms with the radically different world in which we live today and make adjustments that leave children prepared to live in light of current realities.

Educators frequently generalize that children from poorer homes are not as successful academically as are children from well-to-do families. This is not a rule, but a generalization. The genetic capacity to learn exists in both poor and wealthy children. Nevertheless, the generalization that children from lower socioeconomic homes do not experience the same degree of success on standardized tests as their well-to-do classmates is an undeniable fact that must be addressed. There is a need for a different approach that does more than encourage poorer families to purchase costly compensatory programs.

One simple solution is for the school system to move out of the agrarian past into the modern era. Few children now help parents harvest their crops. In order to change this effectively and to address the serious problem of inequality in our society that falls out along socioeconomic lines, the school system and its unions in particular must come to terms with the implications of the data about schools which is now well established.

It is fashionable for unions to make disparaging remarks regarding the use of information based on standardized tests. They go to great lengths to discredit large-scale testing as exemplified by an article in Canada's *National Post* newspaper, dated September 6, 2007: "Frank Bruseker, president of the Alberta Teachers' Association, scoffed at the notion of standardized testing. . . . 'Standardized tests are very effective at measuring the size of the homes in the neighborhood—and that's about all they measure.'"

Studies demonstrate repeatedly that Bruseker's opinion is, in fact, partially correct. The Fraser Institute is a think tank that analyzes test data across Canada and rank-orders school by their performance based on *raw score test results*. Using their ratings, which included two of Canada's larger school districts—Edmonton and Calgary—each with about 100,000 students, schools were rated on a ten-point scale, with ten representing the highest level of student performance.

We used these ratings and found that schools serving families with an annual family income of less than $60,000 had an average rating score of 4.1 in Calgary and 4.3 in Edmonton. In schools where families enjoyed an annual family income in excess of $110,000, both the Calgary and Edmonton schools averaged a rating of 8.0. This means that Bruseker's claim is partially correct, as the correlation between family income and the size of one's house is surely statistically significant and very high.

However, it is also incorrect because the Fraser Institute's study demonstrates that the test is not only very good at measuring the size of the house, or in this case wealth, but it is also equally good at measuring student achievement. Because he and the unions which he represents are unwilling to face this fact, the educational system is not addressing the needs of a large segment of the population. As a result, our nations' schools, which are unwilling to meet the educational needs of students coming from poorer families, are reinforcing social inequality.

This inequality is what the teachers' unions should be focused on. Making standardized tests—that expose inequalities in student achievement—into a villain simply because unions fear that they will also expose weak teachers through their evaluation process, is wrong headed and socially unconscionable. Instead of standing for justice, the unions become purveyors of injustice which is simply wrong headed. The unions' fear of having teachers evaluated on the basis of student achievement is getting in the way of being advocates for *equal opportunity and fairness* for students.

Alexander et al. (2001) discovered a fascinating insight into development of inequality based on a student's socioeconomic status (SES). They found that student achievement over a five-year period for low, medium, and high SES was relatively equal. In other words, each of these subgroups of students learned equally well as long as they were in school and not on a long vacation leave. SES was not a factor in a student's ability to learn. Children from poor families with smaller homes learned at the same rate as their peers from wealthier families and larger homes.

However, SES becomes a factor in learning due to our practice of granting students a long summer recess. In reading, children from high SES homes gained significantly more during summer vacations than the other two groups, presumably because both parents were not in the work force and had greater flexibility to take their children to the library for accessing reading material. Livingston (2018) reported that 18 percent of American students came from homes with a stay-at-home parent while the other was working. Decades earlier this was not the norm. The number of family members working outside the home has increased dramatically as families endeavor to retain our standard of living.

High SES students also benefit from participating in other enriching summer activities. Their family's ability to travel and experience more geographic regions of the world benefit children when they are connecting with what is learned at school. These students are also more likely to attend costly summer camps, where reading and use of technology are likely part of the activity. The Education Commission of the States reported in its June 2009 circular on "Summer Learning" that "only 4 percent of youth from the lowest income bracket participate in summer camps, as compared to 18 percent of the highest-income youth." In short, high SES students are less likely to experience a summer recess devoid of academic activity.

Miller (2007) captures the essence of this issue using a water-tap metaphor:

> During the school year, children in both affluent and lower-income communities benefit from what is known as the "faucet theory": Learning resources are turned on for all children during the school year. But in the summertime, the faucet is turned off. While all families want to provide the best for their children, there are significant differences between the resources middle-income families and communities can offer their children and what lower-income families and communities can offer. Even though low-income working families typically spend a higher portion of their income on child care than parents in more affluent families even those with multiple low-wage jobs cannot cover the high tuition fees that are typical of many summer day and overnight camps. (P7/8)

Quinn and Polikoff (2017) determined that "students' achievement scores declined over summer vacation by one month's worth of school-year learning" (n.p.). Oxford Learning (https://www.oxfordlearning.com/summer-learning-loss-and-how-to-prevent-it/) on June 7, 2019, reported:

- 2.6 months of math skills are lost over the summer
- 2 months of reading are lost over the summer
- 6 weeks are spent re-learning old material in the fall to make up for summer learning loss.

Further, Ramos (2011) reported summer learning loss relative to year-round school and found that students in settings with a year-round calendar statistically outperformed students with traditional calendars in a school-within-a-school setting in mathematics.

Arne Duncan, U.S. Secretary for Education appeared on the June 5, 2014, WNCP (at 92.3 and located in North Carolina) radio's daily call-in show—*The Sound of Ideas*—regarding how much of what students learn slips away during the long summer break. His belief is that combating the "summer slide" requires more time in school than students currently receive: "If we're serious about ending the cycles of poverty and social failure, the traditional calendar, six, six and a half hours a day, five days a week, nine months a year, is insufficient if we're serious [that] the traditional is insufficient for some children."

Chapter 12

BENEFITS OF SUMMER LEARNING

Little (2009) reminds us that more than 50 percent of school-aged children's waking hours are spent outside of school and that there are multiple benefits to students when they participate in summer programs. Specifically, they situate youth in safe environments; prevent youth from engaging in delinquent activities; teach youth general and specific skills, beliefs, and behaviors; and provide opportunities for youth to develop relationships with peers and mentors. These benefits enhance learning because they also can equip students with the skills necessary to be effective learners and leaders. In other words, summer learning reduces the potential for unsupervised children getting into trouble.

Huggins (2013) summarized his perception regarding the value of summer learning by noting how this extra body of time summer represents is too full of opportunity for our educational system to let it sit unused. He reported that eleven school districts in Colorado, Massachusetts, New York, Connecticut, and Tennessee, with support from the Ford Foundation, provided 300 hours of summer learning time to 20,000 students. The mold is breaking! Perhaps there will be some re-writing of the rules which disadvantage so many children from low SES homes.

Absent in the research are findings that the extended summer learning gap does not impact subgroup populations. The educational system's slavish adherence to an extended summer vacation is unfair to a large segment of the population, and continuing such an approach merely demonstrates how schools disregard its clients' educational needs. Students' need for learning is subjugated by people's desire to enjoy a long summer vacation, and considering how this long-standing practice handicaps low SES students, disregarding this unfairness is a form of malpractice.

One superintendent explored alternatives to this pattern by reviewing several forms of year-round education. This term does not mean that students attend school year-round, even though early in our schooling history some cities adopted this plan with significant immigrant populations requiring instruction in the English language. Schooling for these children was available for up to eleven months a year. Rather, this superintendent's exploration was focused merely on instituting many short breaks scattered throughout the year, with students still attending for the same number of days.

A school trustee, whose husband taught school in the district, approached this superintendent threatening his future employment if he persisted in making this year-round approach a topic of public study and discussion. The long summer vacation was a job perk for teachers that the trustee did not want to be abandoned, and further discussions by this superintendent would constitute a career-limiting move.

The problem faced by many school authorities is that they have relegated too much management of their schools to the teachers' unions, who are not motivated to serve clients' needs first and foremost. The school calendar is frequently enshrined within collective agreements specifying specific dates when schools will be closed, including provision for a long summer vacation. This is a significant perk for teachers coveted by many within the general population.

Fortunately, some school districts understand the disadvantage experienced by a subgroup of students, and are extending their educational programs into the summer months for remediation and enrichment. In most instances, there is an added cost because students are attending school for an additional number of days. Whether these districts are using grants or cutting other services to pay for this extended time, they are demonstrating a commitment to their clients which should be expanded.

Educators and politicians should be advocating for a change to a concept that is outdated and unfair. Perpetuating a culture disadvantaging a segment of our student population is another example of how education lacks a service orientation. Changing this perk may generate conflict between management and workers; however, needs of our clients should prevail over the self-interests of those who are providing educational services.

As with so many educational issues, information must be made available to the public so they acquire greater understanding of concerns. Without this information accompanied by extensive public discussion, self-interest prevails. Naturally this discussion will include the matter of who controls the education system. Is it the trustees, who are elected to ensure students' needs are effectively and efficiently addressed, or has control been turned over to a union contract where losing a perk requires costly compensation?

KEY POINTS

- Students from economically disadvantaged homes are more negatively impacted by long periods of summer vacation than socially and economically advantaged students

- If we believe that a well-educated citizenry is paramount for future economic success, then we must reconsider traditional approaches to the school year which may not be serving us very well.
- Learning loss is exacerbated by extensive year-end shut-down activities and year-opening activities, including time needed to review learning that was forgotten.
- During the school year, children in both affluent and lower-income communities benefit from what is known as the "faucet theory": Learning resources are turned on for all children during the school year.
- Summer learning reduces the forgetting rate and potential for students to experience social problems.

Chapter 13

Coaches Are Not Evaluators

> We cannot trust even well-intentioned people if they are not good at what they are doing. Effective, highly interactive cultures incorporate pressure and high support; it is impossible not to notice whether someone is doing great work or bad work. Because people in these cultures know that improvement is tough going and that disagreement is a normal part of any change, they are more inclined and prepared to confront it. Students, parents and colleagues know when bad teaching is being tolerated.
>
> —Michael Fullan, *Leadership and Sustainability: System Thinkers in Action*

Schools are a social enterprise with numerous interactions between the home and educators. Conflict can readily occur when these interactions are rooted in a problem between parents and their child's teacher resulting in a tendency for parents to assume that school staff will stick together. Concerns with how their child is instructed are one of the more contentious issues fragmenting a productive home and school relationship.

Well-intentioned school principals are in an untenable position today, and it seriously degrades their school's effectiveness. On the one hand, they are required to lead through influence and trust while, on the other, they are to assess and evaluate in ways that could end a colleague's career. Is it realistic to think that a person can cultivate friendship and support one day while confronting mediocrity on the next?

Coaching teachers, a fundamental responsibility assigned to principals, requires a relationship of integrity developed over time, but can this bond be cultivated when both parties *know assessment devoid of personal feeling is also required*? This chapter argues that it is *unrealistic to expect principals to play both roles* and that by insisting on it, we have opted for an approach that ultimately *tolerates bad teaching*. The current model is an example of teachers rather than students being atop education's pyramidal pinnacle.

THE ROLE OF RELATIONSHIPS IN INFLATED ASSESSMENT

Earlier, we described a concern with teachers' propensity to inflate grades. Teachers spend all of their time coaching students on ways to succeed and to reach their potential; then, we ask them to assume the mantle of an evaluator who will assess the degree to which learning is achieved. Consequently, significant levels of *grade inflation* occur, and the whole process of having teachers acting as the *sole evaluator* of their own students is called into question. This is one of the reasons the educational system has to incorporate *large-scale assessment and empirical evidence*.

Teaching is a relational activity and being the conveyor of bad news is difficult. Informing students that they are failing to attain grade-level standards and how repeating a course would be in their best interests is difficult. Social promotion, a common practice since the 1980s, alleviated the problem and enabled the school *to avoid being held accountable for student achievement* and for the emotional trauma of separating students out from a peer group: albeit with a group functioning at a similar stage in their learning.

Relationships interfere with objectivity. Society, in general, understands this reality and sets up criteria to take it into account. For example, obtaining a driver's license is a significant milestone on the path to adulthood. Parents are often involved in coaching their children to become good drivers. Accountability is high because the parent is obviously concerned about the safety of their child, but they are also concerned about the possibility of damage to their vehicle and the potential impact this will have on their insurance coverage. Motivation to provide good coaching is at a high level, and many parents wisely reach out to others, such as a driver training instructor, for assistance.

Our governments do not accept that a parent's high sense of accountability and motivation to ensure their son or daughter learns to drive well is a reason to entrust them with the responsibility to determine if their child is ready for a driver's license. On the contrary, qualifying for a driver's license requires passing a standardized test as well as a practical road experience with an examiner, who makes the final determination about readiness. A passing certificate, or driver's license, is only granted when potentially biased interpersonal relationships are removed. Even driver trainers as coaches are considered too close to the student to give the final verdict.

In sports, the usual model in managing teams is to separate the coaching role from the selection process. Coaches manage the team in the sense of determining who will play what position and which players will be on the field of play at a given point in time. Between games they instruct players on how they can perform more effectively and use a variety of strategies to maximize the player's motivation.

However, someone with a higher level of responsibility and a greater sense of objectivity decides who can wear the team uniform. General managers coordinate player selection and de-selection processes including trades. These processes undoubtedly incorporate coaches' opinions, but the general manager is responsible to provide the team's coach or manager with the best player talent given the resources available. The general manager is also responsible to the team's president or owner to manage the coaches so performance throughout the organization is maximized.

In some areas of the private sector, the coach and evaluator are conflated, but this is normal because the bottom line (profit) acts as an independent *arbiter of performance*. There is a far more discernible bottom line where profit and loss are the significant measures. An owner is compelled to move quickly when employees are not doing the job efficiently and effectively. Underperformance in the private sector has the capacity to imperil the entire operation so accountability is relatively simple and straightforward.

Teachers and school administrators, along with most other public employees, have been successful at resisting this model of accountability. *Educators focus more on process than on student outcomes, especially those related to academic achievement.* Too frequently they look to blame the home for ineffective parenting or to government for providing insufficient funding. Blame is assigned to the student for his or her lack of motivation rather than to the teachers' lack of effort and teaching talent.

Principals' lack of bottom-line measurement data related to student outcomes is reduced to *measuring the processes teachers use in their classroom.*

They measure these against their own standards on how well these processes are applied, but their judgments are clouded by their own philosophy regarding which teacher practices are the most suitable for student success. Within all of this activity, as well intentioned as it may be, there is a greater personal problem that principals must overcome.

While fulfilling their *coaching role*, principals concentrate on building trust with teachers by forging strong relationships. Like teachers, when assessing their students, principals believe they provided an excellent job of coaching in preparation for the evaluation. Recognizing shortcomings in their clients' abilities can be interpreted as proving their coaching efforts were not effective. Not surprisingly, they see some scant evidence of effective teaching *and inflate the degree to which the teacher actually can apply it consistently.*

THE "BACK SCRATCH" EFFECT

The entire teacher supervision process is tainted further by a wrongheaded focus involved in principals' evaluations when involving the very same people he or she is evaluating, namely teachers. In essence, this approach is characterized by *"I'll scratch your back if you scratch mine."* This conflict of interest should, by itself, be sufficient to end the practice *unless the educational system incorporates a check and balance approach with a principal evaluation model that focuses primarily on student outcomes in the school.*

Such a model, where coaches evaluate their direct reports, is also an issue in school district offices. One superintendent commented that she instituted a five-level-scale evaluation model for her assistant superintendents. It was the first-time empirical data sources gleaned from client satisfaction surveys were used in the district. These evaluations were not just a pass/fail model but utilized the five-level-scale ranging from "excellent" to "less than satisfactory."

Based on the data as well as her observations, she identified several areas with each subordinate where work performance was solid but not demonstrating "excellence." On this basis, the overall performance was rated as "very good." These assistant superintendents were not pleased that their evaluations left them with ratings below "excellent." It was standard practice in surrounding districts to evaluate senior staff as "excellent," and these specific senior staff worried that a rating less than the norm could negatively impact their career opportunities.

In essence, senior staff believed an "excellent" performance rating was their *entitlement. The politically correct action was to provide the norm.* Introducing empirical data made it impossible for evaluators to come to a conclusion where everyone is assessed "excellent" because the data differentiated employees on the basis of performance. This superintendent blazed a trail of nonconformity and she would pay the price. Those who were disgruntled with her objective evaluation formed a small, disloyal alliance and waited until it was their turn to evaluate her and settle the score.

At the school level, *the problem is that principals provide high ratings for their teachers because teachers will rate them when their leadership will be evaluated by district leaders.* This pattern of behavior is replicated further up the hierarchy as assistant superintendents want high evaluations from their principals when the superintendent is conducting their performance reviews. Similarly, the superintendent is anticipating loyalty from underlings when the school board is reviewing their leadership. Everyone is looking to have "their back scratched." Once again, standards suffer because performance levels are inflated.

The proof of how ineffective the current evaluation process for educators is can be found in the de-selection data. The current model is not weeding out ineffective teachers because standards are too low. Principals are not "calling a spade a spade." The educational system places too much emphasis on staff relationships to the detriment of student outcomes. In the area of teacher supervision, *the educational system is arranged in a way that not only falls short of the student's best interest; it is arranged in a way that runs counter to the student's best interest.*

This unfortunate reality, *where relationships blind objectivity,* supports the union's primary objective, which is to look after the welfare of their members. They are not committed to looking after the best interests of the system's clients by ridding classrooms of ineffective practitioners. Neither are they supportive of using large-scale testing programs to identify weak teachers who may need to feel some pressure to improve. *Unions cannot pursue simultaneously the best interests of their members and the system's clients.* Their conflict of interest is self-evident.

This is depressingly easy to illustrate. One superintendent spoke of his experience with the union at the negotiating table. The union's position was that all teachers are "excellent," but that *management is to blame for the poor level of service from some because teachers were not placed properly where they can excel.* The teacher might function more effectively if there were fewer students in the class or with fewer students demonstrating special needs. The union's perspective was that the superintendent was not making sufficient effort to place the teacher in situations where their capacity for excellence could be displayed.

Why are state politicians so complacent about this clearly inadequate system of staff supervision? One of the most obvious reasons is that their governance structure also operates without adequate concern for the bottom line. Public sector enterprises share a common ethos, and politicians looking to "right the ship" in education would have to "right their own" first. In other words, they would have to tackle the self-centeredness of their own government's unions first, and then deal directly with the ensuing conflict.

Well-intentioned incompetence is a major issue imperiling our society. Courage is a virtue we want all politicians to demonstrate, but it is rare, particularly when their political careers are always at stake. This explains their propensity for funding projects those who elected them favor, and it explains why they are reticent to deal with complex and nebulous issues like staff supervision in schools, even though they might personally consider this an issue worthy of their attention.

School district officials associated with educational leadership are fairly knowledgeable about superintendent Michelle Rhee's efforts to "weed-out" poor teachers in Washington, D.C. She was known for her ability to remove poor teachers! In the end, the political heat her employers experienced was beyond their ability to endure. Having to choose between policies that championed students and those which favored interest groups, the school board waivered and then capitulated. Ms. Rhee went on to other educational endeavors.

Rhee was successful at least at one level: she used empirical evidence to show how bad the situation was and who the weak teachers were. *The critical point in this chapter is that coaches cannot evaluate unless they use empirical data to influence the evaluation process.* Data provides the basis for differentiated evaluations and the *likelihood of tension in working relationships.*

For principals to serve as effective team evaluators, they have to resort to empirical evidence, which is best for students in any case. Any other method of evaluation will lead to dysfunction. Even a simple statement that appears to have a negative connotation may produce conflict or even sever a relationship. Once the relationship is damaged, the principal will surely experience difficulty when it comes time for their assessment from the district office. The solution is to introduce higher levels of objectivity into the process.

REVEALING HIDDEN SECRETS OF A POOR EVALUATION SYSTEM

The media is now beginning to educate the public and provide for much greater transparency in the school system so that an informed public can influence developments in the school. *Waiting for "Superman,"* a pro-education reform documentary, indicated how, in Illinois, 1 out of every 57 doctors lost his or her license to practice medicine; one out of every 97 lawyers lost their license to practice law; and in many major cities, only 1 out of 1,000 teachers is fired for performance-related reasons (https://www.huffpost.com/entry/factchecking-waiting-for-_b_802900).

Newsmedia are now investigating the issue, and some of their findings are summarized below:

> Though it has been well-documented that the cases drag on for years and can cost a district hundreds of thousands of dollars—they last an average of 502 days and cost $216,588—the database shows that 3020-a hearings rarely result in termination. Of the more than 2,000 cases brought in the last five years, just 167 teachers were fired, the vast majority in New York City. Only 38 cases brought by schools districts upstate and on Long Island ended in termination, though a number are still undecided because it takes so long for a case to be completed. Statewide, 593 cases were simply settled and another 164 were withdrawn or consolidated. (N.p.) (https://www.timesunion.com/local/article/Solving-puzzle-of-bad-teachers-2232004.php.)

> In Chicago, the number of teachers dismissed for poor performance between 2005 and 2008 was 0.1 percent. During that same time frame, Toledo, Ohio, dismissed just .01 percent, and Akron, Ohio and Denver, Colorado did not dismiss any. Instead of getting rid of poor performers, principals try to shuffle them into other schools and districts—a process known as the "dance of the lemons" by many schools today. (N.p.) (https://www.publicschoolreview.com/blog/why-it-can-take-six-years-to-fire-an-inappropriate-or-ineffective-teacher)

Anderson (2013), a writer for the *New York Times*, reported that roughly 100 percent of teachers in Florida were deemed "effective" or "highly effective" in the most recent evaluations. Incredibly, teacher evaluations in 2011 typically involved a *single observation of about twenty minutes*. In Tennessee, 98 percent of teachers were judged to be "at expectations" and in Michigan, 98 percent of teachers were rated "effective" or better. An official with the National Council on Teacher Quality conceded how the current situation was alarming necessitating a significant culture shift in education.

What is the cultural shift that must happen? Even though some teacher evaluations are partly contingent on student test scores, they are mostly focused on principals' assessments acquired through their own observations of teachers. There is a need to abandon a culture where almost all teachers are considered *above average*.

Anderson points out how this problem of low standards is exacerbated by the involvement of evaluators "who generally are not detached managerial types and can be loath to give teachers low marks" (n.p.). Education is strengthened by having relational people working with students: it is weakened by requiring these well-intentioned people to "bell the cat" of mediocre colleagues. This emphasis on relationships is why there is not a substantial increase in the percentage of teachers who are removed from the classroom. This may also be why some principals write their teachers' evaluations based on one twenty-minute observation.

When Anderson informed Grover J. Whitehurst, director of the Brown Center on Education Policy at the Brookings Institution that very few teachers were deemed "ineffective," he responded, "It would be an unusual profession that at least 5 percent are not deemed ineffective" (n.p.). Evaluating and developing talent is the most important management function in the educational system, whether it is occurring in the classroom with students by their teachers or with teachers by their principals. However, *low standards are endemic in the educational system* even though we claim that education is vital for our nation's future well-being.

Mellon (2010) explored the problem of low standards and asked why, in the past, teachers were rarely let go because of poor classroom performance? In an interview with Houston Superintendent, Terry Grier, who led nine school districts over twenty-five years, Grier theorized, "I think some principals accept mediocrity because they don't want to go through the battle with the teachers' union or through the process of aggressively recruiting others" (n.p.). *There is a need to apply pressure on those who lack the courage to combat mediocrity.*

The term "pressure" is an emotionally charged concept within education. Fullan (2009) expands our thinking about the value of using pressure to motivate activity:

> The opposite of pressure is not no pressure. No pressure is complacency. No pressure is inertia's other best friend. . . . A focused sense of urgency gets people's attention; partnership and peer learning increase support, but also pressure from successful cases (if it is done in circumstances similar to ours); transparency of data makes it even more evident who is successful and who is not. (N.p.)

Fullan goes on to explain differences in positive and negative pressure, but a critical point is that pressure is not an either/or situation. Pressure can be very motivational and is enhanced by transparency: "It exposes not only results, but practices that produce results. It generates specific, precise, visually clear images of what works. It is accessible for all as it takes all excuses off the table" (n.p.).

Incorporating objective data, such as student achievement on tests, applies additional pressure to raise teaching standards, but this method is not without its own hiccups. Such a program is still managed by people within the system and can still be politically manipulated as evidenced by Anderson's report on one American county. Cut scores from test data used in evaluating teachers were set relatively high, but when only 78 percent of teachers were deemed "highly effective" or "effective," and when they saw how lenient other neighboring districts in the county were, they reset them much lower. Ultimately, 99.4 percent of teachers were rated "effective" or "highly effective" (n.p.).

A NEW FRONTIER IN TEACHER EVALUATION

Earlier in this book, we indicated utilizing test scores in teacher evaluation systems is a relatively new endeavor. There will be problems not unlike those evident in how teachers assess students. *Misuse by some does not mean disuse generally.* There is more promise for fairness than what occurs when educational systems rely exclusively on the teachers' assessments of students' work in the classroom. The significant degree of grade inflation that occurs when a teacher-student relationship influences assessments is a concern.

Some school systems frequently rely on external tests for generating marks used in decisions regarding scholarships and placements into prestigious universities. This methodology requires a consistent application of cut scores so that there is adherence to standards and fixed goal posts are not moving. Students may feel disadvantaged by not being able to influence marks through strategies in compliant behavior, but they benefit from having their learning assessed by an unbiased process. *Fairness to students* is enhanced.

Undoubtedly, teacher unions will continue to denounce inclusion of test scores in evaluating teachers. Introducing measures of empirical data decreases their opportunity to challenge ratings of poor performance in the classroom. Even though teaching processes observed by evaluators continue to comprise most of the final evaluation, there finally is a shift underway to consider learner outcomes. *Learning, then, is no longer the sole responsibility of the student, and this shift, by itself, is a major revolution in education.*

However, this revolution presents a problem for politicians. Their electability is threatened when they adopt an allegiance to students, *who cannot vote*. In New York State, for example, complaints quickly surfaced in 2014 when results on the new Common Core tests were released. In New York City, 26 percent of students in third through eighth grade passed the tests in English and 30 percent passed in mathematics. These new tests emphasized deep analysis and creative problem-solving rather than the traditional approach of short answers and memorization. In the previous year, when the old tests were used, 47 percent of city students passed in English and 60 percent in mathematics.

Across the state, the downward shift was similar: 31 percent of students passed the exams in reading and mathematics, compared with 55 percent in reading, and 65 percent in mathematics the previous year. These poor results were chilling news for politicians, who sanctioned the previous testing program where standards were being systematically reduced in order to qualify for improvement grants under the George Bush presidency's No Child Left Behind legislation.

Their deception exposed, politicians reacted immediately as leaders of both political parties in the New York State Legislature called on the state to back away from plans to use those exams to grade teacher performance. A news report in the *New York Times* on February 4, 2014 (https://www.nytimes.com/2014/02/05/nyregion/a-call-to-ignore-exam-results-when-evaluating-educators.html) captured the political paranoia:

> In synchronized statements, Democratic leaders of the State Assembly joined Republicans in the State Senate to propose that the tests, which are aligned with the new curriculum standards known as the Common Core, be excluded, for now, from the state's new teacher evaluation system, which Gov. Andrew M. Cuomo signed into law in 2012.
>
> The proposal will involve altering the law, which requires that the state test results be used for at least 20 percent of a teacher's evaluation. Other factors, like principals' observations and locally designed tests, make up the bulk of the grade. Teachers who earn the lowest mark—"ineffective"—two years in a row are at risk of losing their jobs.
>
> The change would require backtracking on one of the governor's earliest legislative victories. But it also could give him an antidote to mounting complaints over the Common Core in a re-election year. Mr. Cuomo has already said he would name a panel to recommend changes to what he called a "flawed" rollout of the Common Core. (N.p.)

The key phrase in this article—"an antidote to mounting complaints over the Common Core in a re-election year"—demonstrates succinctly how *politicians perpetuate unfairness to their students in deference to teachers and their unions.* Too frequently an election causes politicians to subjugate education's clients' best interests simply because they are not on the voters' lists. For a period of time, the New York school system will revert to an evaluation system based on principals' evaluations, as deeply flawed as this process is.

This hesitation to proceed with the most challenging aspect of attaching consequences with performance, as required in the U.S. national effort of the Race to the Top initiative, provides a clear example regarding how politicians align with their most powerful special interest group: teachers' unions. New York is a Democrat state, and teacher unions support Democrat candidates overwhelmingly. From 1989 through the 2014 election cycle, the NEA spent over $92 million on political campaign contributions, 97 percent of which went to Democrats (https://en.wikipedia.org/wiki/National_Education_Association).

Similar delays in incorporating student achievement on system tests into teacher evaluations are reported in 2014 for California and Iowa. Both states voted Democrat in the 2012 Presidential election. *It is not an overstatement to say that the power of teachers' unions is persuasive and pervasive.*

Nevertheless, progress in attaching higher levels of accountability to teachers for improving student achievement is being made across the U.S. One think tank, The National Council on Teacher Quality, reports a successful trend using data for years 2009, 2011, and 2013 (https://files.eric.ed.gov/fulltext/ED598961.pdf).

- Requiring *annual* evaluation of all teachers: 15, 25, and 28 states.
- Student achievement is the *preponderant* criterion in teacher evaluation: 4, 13, and 20 states.
- Evidence of effectiveness is the basis of teacher *tenure* decisions: 0, 8, and 19 states.

Making use of empirical data is a critical aspect for reforming valid and reliable teacher evaluations; however, there remains a requirement to resolve the issue that coaches should not also be the evaluator. School administrators, wanting to achieve the highest level of teamwork possible, risk many negative consequences when they provide staff with multilevel evaluations (e.g., five-point scale) including one that severs the relationship.

During a discussion on this issue with superintendents, one told of his experience with principals. The school district had a contractual provision that teachers on the substitute list held seniority over non-hired applicants if they produced a "satisfactory" evaluation on fourteen out of seventeen elements of instruction on two consecutive substituting placements involving three or more days. His district was surrounded by other districts and many of the teachers in the substitute pool accepted assignments in all of them but were routinely passed over when they were hiring.

This superintendent was concerned that principals would have too low expectations during their evaluations of these long-term substitutes. These principals were anxious that the teachers' union would target them and the superintendent's concerns materialized, as virtually all evaluations met the minimum requirement for hiring. The superintendent implemented a check and balance approach by designating a district officer to conduct all second assessments after the substitute teacher had received the initial qualifying report.

Many substitute teachers qualified for the minimal standard and the district was forced to hire them even though outstanding teachers from other places or from universities were bypassed. The critical point, however, is that the district officer shielded the district from having to hire many teachers who were not highly talented but were able to obtain satisfactory reports from principals who might never have them placed in their school.

This superintendent's experience reiterates how teacher evaluations should be undertaken by someone external to the school. District staff want to be known as instructional leaders and including *teacher evaluations* as part of their job description is a higher-order activity. Their involvement not only raises the profile of district staff, but it also signals the school district's commitment for having highly competent teachers. Incorporating this responsibility cannot be perceived as an add-on but a basic leadership function required of all administrators.

Earlier in this book, Edmonton school district's success was heralded for improving student achievement the longer they were enrolled within the district. A follow-up conversation with the superintendent revealed his commitment to instructional leadership. During his four-year tenure, 7,500 classrooms were visited after discussions with the principal when he asked three basic questions: What will we see? What won't we see? What is your coaching plan for this teacher?

A school district with 100,000 students can easily distract central office staff from their instructional leadership functions by making "administrivia" their primary mandate. These visits consumed a significant amount of time but ensuring that schools were improving was this superintendent's central purpose. His slogan, "failure is not an option" was a driving force and, *when a school was not improving, this superintendent intervened in the school's autonomy by designing the school's professional development program.*

Parents were the beneficiaries of this passionate leadership *because their children were winning.* Some people may espouse that a politically correct posture is to have school staff prepare their professional development so that ownership is enhanced. Instead, this superintendent believed there is a sense of urgency so that some students are not disadvantaged to accommodate politically correct activity. Years later on March 1, 2010, U.S. president

Obama made a related statement to the U.S. Chamber of Commerce, "Our kids only get one chance at an education and we need to get it right."

Principals may be well-intentioned people but their track record in evaluating teachers is abysmal. Mutually beneficial back-scratching dominates our schools' politically correct culture where people other than students occupy the pyramidal pinnacle. Teacher evaluation is so important that it must be the focus of all administrators selected for leadership functions in the school district offices. Achieving excellent teacher services for our children requires a two-pronged approach. The principal's work should be focused on *developing teacher talent* while the district office is responsible for providing an arms-length function of *evaluating teacher performance.*

This chapter conveys the simple message that teachers are not equally proficient even though binary evaluations (pass/fail) make it appear so. Most schools have more than one teacher working with the same grade and school administrators are obligated to assist interested parents in selecting the most appropriate placement. Listening to a parent's description of how their child learns best is one obvious consideration.

One principal employed another function during twelve years of school leadership when he met with teachers every reporting period to discuss each child's educational progress. The detailed notes in his "Pupil Progress" binder provided valuable information for constructing appropriate class lists for a new term. Standardized test results provide another significant set of information, albeit controversial and requiring discreet presentation. While the documentation remains within the school, parents should be able to see summaries of class, school, and provincial/state test results.

Incorporating this process ensures that parents will be strong allies in the school's educational endeavors.

KEY POINTS

- We cannot trust even well-intentioned people if they are not good at what they are doing.
- Education is plagued by a model that places the school principal in a dual role as a teacher coach and evaluator.
- Relationships cause grade inflation to be endemic in education including when principals evaluate their teachers.

- Staff evaluation processes produce a culture dominated by mutual "back scratching."
- Use of empirical evidence in staff evaluations is changing the status quo; however, many politicians wilt in their commitments to incorporate empirical data into staff evaluations.
- Teacher evaluations should be conducted by someone outside of the school which provides excellent opportunity for district staff to engage in instructional leadership.

Chapter 14

Disregarding Our Best and Brightest

The school system has a long-standing history of interrupting the educational progress of students who are falling behind and who require additional time to attain a reasonable level of achievement for success in their workplace. Indeed, dealing first and foremost with academically weak students may be characterized as the school system's *moral imperative* with teachers focused on bringing these students up to grade level (Fullan 2003). Approximately 17 percent of students in K-9 were retained across the province at least one grade prior to entering grade ten in high school.

Parents should be aware that this concern about weaker students somewhat displaces the attentiveness we should have for our more talented learners who are hampered by a "glass ceiling." In Alberta's ten-year study, only 1 percent of students below high school were accelerated, and many times more students were assessed *by teachers* as "below" rather than "above" grade level.

Schwartz (2016) reported a similarly bleak assessment across the United States using a nation-wide survey regarding programming, policies, funding, and teacher qualifications:

> Of the responding districts, only 1.7% of elementary districts provided subject acceleration while only 0.2% provided opportunities for students to accelerate one whole grade or more. On the middle school level, 2.4% provided subject acceleration, and 0.3% allowed for acceleration by grade. High school acceleration opportunities were primarily provided through AP, IB, and dual enrollment courses. (p.14)

A low incidence of acceleration by grade is a critical finding. There is confusion that intervention through academic acceleration applies mostly to children of wealth. The truth is that giftedness cuts across gender, ethnicity, social and economic background, and geographic location (Colangelo et al. 2004). As educators, we chafe at lock-step approaches with all students at the same place following the same pace. These authors summarize the problem by indicating how many teachers and administrators want to provide high-ability students the flexibility to move at the pace of their talents. But these educators—teachers and school administrators—want support and validation.

Absence of *early standardized testing* is one reason why talented achievers are inadequately identified. Standardized testing provides educators and parents with a viable screen for validating a student's strength. A teacher's opinion in a culture so dominated by the moral imperative creates hesitancy for taking action and declaring that a student will benefit from an accelerated instructional program. Evidence from an early standardized assessment can kickstart discussions for personalizing a student's program commensurate with their potential.

Knowing when to initiate acceleration is a stumbling block for early years because teachers are hesitant to make the decision without corroboration from others. Lupkowski-Shoplik (2004) suggests,

> Earlier is better, at least socially. It becomes more difficult as students get older and become more involved in activities—it's harder to leave those old friends behind. This becomes a bigger and bigger issue when a student reaches high school. There are lots of kids who wait until high school to skip a grade, however, and they do it successfully. (N.p.)

Our reasoning regarding leaving old friends behind appears more focused on social than educational needs.

Insufficient academic data is a significant deterrent for early acceleration. A standardized testing program in primary grades provides insight into students' weaknesses and strengths. Educators have the option for waiting until end-of-year tests provide confirmation to initiate discussions with parents. A grade one student, for example, could take the grade one and/or two tests, and students in subsequent years could also take multiple tests. These assessments provide educators with valuable data for planning students' academic program.

This additional information from an early testing program presents the school system with an opportunity to change a culture so dominated by the "glass ceiling." Increasing assessment data facilitates wiser decisions for accommodating the opposite ends of the achievement continuum and trigger thoughtful actions, including both deceleration and acceleration. Parents, too, benefit by having quantifiable information regarding their child's potential.

HISTORY OF ACCELERATION

Historically, there were times when grade placements were more readily adjusted. The one-room schoolhouse let students learn at their own pace because it provided education to students of many different ages. Teachers knew their students' individual talent and focused on basic skills. Increasing population ended these one-room school houses which were replaced by larger buildings serving more students. Grouping students by age became the usual practice reducing considerations for ability ambition. In this respect, the passage of one-room schools contributed to a lock-step approach for student progression.

Colangelo et al. (2004) outline how more flexible progression through the school system occurred during America's war years:

> During these times of crisis, our leaders tend to recognize that ability and skill matter more than traditions and rules. Just before World War II, The Ohio State University, the University of Illinois, and the University of Chicago all started programs to enroll young college students. During the Korean War, universities responded in a similar way. The Ford Foundation provided scholarship support for students under age 16 to enroll full-time at the university level before joining the military. After this effort ended, the 12 colleges participating in this program continued to accept young students, but they stopped actively recruiting them—or providing special financial aid. The Ford Foundation, however, did something very special in the mid-1950s, which now assists more than one million American students every year. It established the College Board Advanced Placement Program (AP), which allows colleges and universities to offer credit and advanced standing to high school students. In 2004, an amazing 1.9 million AP exams were taken. Those students are the descendants of the fast-moving scholars of the one-room schoolhouses of previous generations. (p.12)

These writers also reported that

> every year, 200,000 seventh-grade and eighth grade students take the SAT or ACT college entrance exams. The majority score as well as high school seniors, who are usually four or five-years older. But the academically stronger members of that pool of 200,000 young test-takers (middle school students)—those who score at or above the average score for high school seniors—are especially gifted. Those students can absorb a whole year's worth of high school in three weeks, researchers say. In fact, a few of the very highest scorers on the SAT, as middle school students, can actually absorb a year's worth of high school in just a week and a half. (p.22)

This finding about how little time is actually required for a gifted student to absorb a year's worth of high school is truly amazing and demonstrates how students' talent is wasted by our slavish adherence to lock-step progression so dominant in our present school system. These writers also proceed to encourage parents to be aware of the gifted student's boredom factor:

> Parents are usually the first to suspect that their child is not challenged in school. A dad may notice that when he provides books or puzzles which challenge his child, the child seems happier. The scientific evidence supporting these parental observations is overwhelming. Students who are carefully selected for early entrance to school generally perform very well, both academically and socially. The reasons for this are clear. By starting school early, an underchallenged child doesn't learn what it's like to be bored. Instead of finding that school is easy and that he can succeed without having to work, a child who is placed in the right classroom, right from the start will learn that striving to improve is a wonderful part of learning. We all know very bright children who grew up to become unmotivated adults. School was too easy, and the lazy way became the accustomed way. By setting challenges early, we can ensure that children who can't wait to read become adolescents who can't wait to learn. (p.16)

In recent decades, teachers' training was more focused on developing ways for enriching a student's program than on watching for signs indicating giftedness, and then initiating plans for acceleration. In these authors' historic endeavor—*A Nation Deceived: How Schools Hold Back America's Brightest Students*—they summarize how *focusing on enrichment is a misplaced endeavor*:

Is enrichment enough? Because enrichment keeps students with their age-peers, teachers don't worry about it harming children socially or emotionally. However, when enrichment for gifted students does not include a faster pace and higher level of work, it is simply not effective as an intervention. Just putting gifted kids together—but not accelerating the curriculum—has minimal academic benefit. The key component is the accelerated curriculum. Sometimes talented students are taught in a separate class, but they're not accelerated. Researchers investigating the effects of this found something stunning. If the talented students were given the same curriculum as the regular class, the effect on their academic performance was zero. There was absolutely no academic benefit to that specially-grouped math class that was not doing advanced math. So, a room full of bright students, without more challenging material, does absolutely nothing academically. If the special group had a differentiated curriculum, there was some academic benefit, but not as much as acceleration. Clearly, the best way to maximize the academic performance of bright students is to maximize the pace and level of the curriculum. (p.22)

CLARIFYING ACCELERATION

Bailey et al. (2004) provide a summary of acceleration as well as a concise set of examples.

> Acceleration is a strategy that allows a student to progress through school at a faster than usual rate and/or younger than typical age. There are several forms of acceleration to consider for any individual student.
> - **Subject acceleration,** where students are promoted to a higher year for one or more of the subjects in which they excel
> - **Grade skipping,** where students are promoted to a higher year for all subjects, for example, Jordan who was moved from Year 1 at the end of one school year into Year 3 at the beginning of the next
> - **Early entry,** which usually means that a gifted child who displays academic and social readiness begins school at a younger age than most other children do
> - **Telescoping,** where a student, or a group of students, completes two years in one, or some similar rapid progression through material
> - **Radical acceleration,** where highly/profoundly gifted students skip several grades, and/or experience several forms of acceleration, during their school years. (N.p.)

Colangelo et al. (2004) clarify the definition further by linking these methods with a student need: "Many researchers consider acceleration to be 'appropriate educational planning. It means matching the level and complexity of the curriculum with the readiness and motivation of the student'" (p.66). Their clarification is crucial to this discussion because, not only is the student's giftedness important, but their attitude through motivation must be a consideration.

These authors reference their provocative report regarding how America has been deceived as well as deceiving the nation's brightest students. Their twenty most critical points are:

1. Acceleration is the most effective curriculum intervention for gifted children.
2. For bright students, acceleration has long-term beneficial effects, both academically and socially.
3. Acceleration is a virtually cost-free intervention.
4. Gifted children tend to be socially and emotionally more mature than their age-mates. For many bright students, acceleration provides a better personal maturity match with classmates.
5. When bright students are presented with curriculum developed for age-peers, they can become bored and unhappy and get turned off from learning.
6. Testing, especially above-level testing (using tests developed for older students), is highly effective in identifying students who would benefit from acceleration.
7. The evidence and mechanisms are available to help schools make good decisions about acceleration so that it is a low-risk/high-success intervention for qualified students. The Iowa Acceleration Scale is a proven, effective instrument for helping schools make decisions about whole-grade acceleration.
8. The 18 types of acceleration available to bright students fall into two broad categories: grade-based acceleration, which shortens the number of years a student spends in the K–12 system, and subject-based acceleration, which allows for advanced content earlier than customary.
9. Entering school early is an excellent option for some gifted students both academically and socially. High-ability young children who enroll early generally settle in smoothly with their older classmates.

10 Gifted students entering college early experience both short-term and long-term academic success, leading to long-term occupational success and personal satisfaction.
11 Many alternatives to full-time early college entrance are available for bright high school students who prefer to stay with age-peers. These include dual enrollment in high school and college, distance education, and summer programs. Advanced Placement (AP) is the best large-scale option for bright students who want to take college-level courses in high school.
12 Very few early college entrants experience social or emotional difficulties. When these do occur, they are usually short-term and part of the adjustment process.
13 Radical acceleration (acceleration by two or more years) is effective academically and socially for highly gifted students.
14 Many educators have been largely negative about the practice of acceleration, despite abundant research evidence for its success and viability.
15 To encourage a major change in America's perceptions of educational acceleration, we will need to use all the engines of change: legislation, the courts, administrative rules, and professional initiatives.
16 Effective implementation of accelerative options for gifted students with disabilities is time and resource intensive.
17 It is important for parents to be fully involved in the decision-making process about their child's acceleration.
18 The few problems that have been experienced with acceleration have stemmed primarily from incomplete or poor planning.
19 Educational equity does not mean educational sameness. Equity respects individual differences in readiness to learn and recognizes the value of each student.
20 The key question for educators is not whether to accelerate a gifted learner but rather how. (p.2)

Using standardized testing for assessing bright students is one of their points (#6) and is consistent with our earlier reference for testing students annually in the early grades. School staff can estimate the approximate achievement levels for students and arrange to include these in writing the appropriate tests. This suggestion provides a cost-effective means for generalizing a student's potential for acceleration.

SOCIAL IMPLICATIONS WITH ACCELERATION

Despite research demonstrating the benefits of accelerating student programming through the school system, little progress is evident. Many myths and understandings prevent educators from breaking out of a rut with gifted students for fear that they will do harm. We sometimes worry that children who skip grades have to leave friends behind. By starting school early, and moving through school with the same class, bright students do not need to leave familiar classmates. They are appropriately placed from their first day of school.

A wrong perception in schooling is how ability is attached to physical age. For centuries, the model for schooling focused on a child's birthdate in relation to the first day of a new school year. Educators determine grade placement using age rather than readiness; yet, we know that significant differences in learning occur. The lock-step approach generally used with students must be replaced by readiness, rather than age, as the main determinant for grade placement.

Colangelo et al. (2004) in their national summary report concluded that

> some argue that acceleration can be harmful to students' self-concept, ability to fit in with older peers, or other social-emotional needs. However, research on acceleration has demonstrated multiple academic benefits to students and suggests that acceleration does not harm students. As the National Work Group on Acceleration determined, there is "no evidence that acceleration has a negative effect on a student's social-emotional development." (p.3)

One website, www.DavidsonGifted.org., dedicated to increasing awareness about the plight of gifted students, responded to the question regarding a potential for social adjustment problems:

> On the contrary, the somewhat surprising finding (given teachers', and some parents', concerns about this matter) is that grade-skipping tends to produce a strong improvement in social adjustment (along with a small gain in self-esteem). As Rogers (2002, p. 168) comments: "It is noteworthy that when these children do move to the higher grade, they are, in fact, more likely to make friends, perhaps because the older children may have similar interests or are slightly more socially mature."

A testimonial from the large-scale Richardson study supports this positive conclusion: "Our files are full of stories about youngsters, named or unnamed, happily studying two, three, even four years ahead of their age-mates. In general, the social adjustment of these precocious youngsters is improved by placing them with their intellectual peers rather than their age-mates." (Daniel 1989, pp. 50–51)

However, this website reminds us that acceleration is not equated with a "magic bullet" for dealing with social concerns:

> While the research evidence shows that acceleration usually has positive consequences for gifted students, it is not a "magic bullet" that cures all academic and social problems.
>
> Acceleration alone may not be enough to eliminate a student's existing social difficulties (in the words of one student: "Acceleration didn't make me a social misfit. I was one already!"), so social skills may need to be addressed separately. Also, a single grade skip is unlikely to be sufficient to satisfy the academic needs of a highly-to profoundly gifted student. (N.p.)

Lee et al. (2012) affirm absence of negative effects from accelerated students noting that

> like mixed ability, heterogeneous students of the same grade, our students rated themselves as fairly competent in initiating, forming and maintaining relationships with other people, including their peers, and believed that they are liked by others. They were hopeful about their future and had a positive overall self-image with low levels of depression. The students in this study were very satisfied with their peer relationships at school and in general. . . . Being labeled as gifted did not bring any negative effects in forming friendships. (p.27)

It is inaccurate to suggest that a gifted student is a social misfit because of their enrollment in the school system. Giftedness does not originate in *grade* one but, rather, during *age* one and thereafter. Interactions with other children, whether these be at family gatherings, playschool, and so on, can contribute to early perceptions of seeing their place in the world differently.

ACADEMIC IMPLICATIONS WITH ACCELERATION

Assisting the understanding of a concept is sometimes best achieved by clarifying what it is not. In this case of acceleration, we emphasize that it is not about forcing a child to acquire skills, knowledge, and understandings, or even socialize with older students, before he or she is ready. Rather, acceleration recognizes that students have different strengths and needs, accommodating these conditions provides interest to excel and motivation to succeed.

Skeptics regarding acceleration may consider this practice as placing stress on students because of "hot-housing" their giftedness. The www.DavidsonGifted.org. website disputes this criticism:

> It is important to realize that acceleration does not mean that gifted students are being made to speed up and learn faster than they are already willing to, but rather that schools are allowing students to progress at something closer to their natural or preferred rate of learning. Holding back gifted students is much more likely to be stressful for them, or harmful in other ways (such as teaching them to "coast" along, which may deny them the opportunity to learn to cope with intellectual challenges). (N.p.)

This response identifies a legitimate concern regarding the potential for coasting through school which must not be overlooked.

When students are granted access to acceleration, the literature reveals positive effects on academic achievement. Kretschmann et al. (2014) compared the academic achievement of elementary school students who skipped a grade with that of their older classmates from the new grade level. After matching the subjects based on family and cultural background, academic capability, age of school enrollment, and economic status, they found that the accelerated students performed at least as well in the new grade level as their nonaccelerated peers. No negative effects were noted, and the skipped students were able to keep up in the new grade level despite having missed a year of instruction.

The www.DavidsonGifted.org. website clarifies this further when clarifying that "acceleration means we have taken off the brakes!" They reference David Elkind's book, *The Hurried Child*, who states:

> Promotion of intellectually gifted children is simply another way of attempting to match the curriculum to the child's abilities, not to accelerate those abilities. What promotion does for intellectually gifted children is to make a better fit between the child's level of development and the curriculum (Elkind, in Smutny et al. 1989, p. 105). That is, Elkind acknowledges the legitimacy of acceleration

as a strategy for the gifted. A characteristic of gifted students is their ability to "reason at a level usually found in a student some years older," so acceleration is a logical way of addressing this. (N.p.)

Again, this website summarizes another study by Karen Rogers' 2002 report demonstrating substantial academic benefits from acceleration:

Gifted early entrants to school were found to be on average six months ahead in their achievement, compared to their age peers, while there were also slight gains in social skills and self-esteem. Studies of single-subject acceleration have found that it produced academic gains of about three-fifths of a year's growth. Telescoping was found to have similarly large positive effects. For concurrent enrolment the academic gains were small but positive. The research on grade skipping has produced very positive findings, with over one additional year's academic achievement resulting, "and the students performed at least as well as their older-aged gifted peers in the new grade level." The Senate Committee (2001, p. xiv) concluded that "there is overwhelming research evidence that appropriate acceleration of gifted students who are socially and emotionally ready usually has highly advantageous outcomes." (N.p.)

Lubinski et al. (2001) studied the satisfaction level of high-ability children who had been accelerated and reported that 71 percent indicated satisfaction with their acceleration experience. Of the participants who reported they were unsatisfied, the majority indicated they would have preferred more acceleration.

The National Association for Gifted Children website (http://www.accelerationinstitute.org/nation_deceived/nd_v1.pdf) summarizes from the American report, *A Nation Deceived: How Schools Hold Back America's Brightest Students*:

Researchers have found that, overall, acceleration influences high-ability students' academic achievement in positive ways, and that these students outperform peers in other areas, including scores on standardized tests, grades in college, and the status of the universities they attend and their later career paths. (N.p.)

This website proceeds to indicate the success of accelerated students after graduation from high school and reported that accelerated students have also been shown to outperform nonaccelerated peers academically in the long term. A longitudinal study of students highly talented in mathematics showed that students who skipped a grade were more likely to obtain graduate degrees, publish work, and receive patents in the STEM areas.

These positive reports on student success are somewhat tempered by The Draper website—www.hoagiesgifted.org/enrichment.htm—which opines that "in spite of the research, most teachers and administrators oppose acceleration and rarely permit it. From what I've seen and read, the reasons include":

- misplaced egalitarianism
- fear, resentment, and dislike of gifted kids (and anyone else who is much smarter than most teachers and administrators)
- ignorance of the research on GKs (Gifted Kids)
- the misinformation about GKs that is widely taught in ed schools and in-service training programs
- fear of alienating the next grade's teachers (as when a 1st grade teacher lets a gifted child study 2nd and 3rd grade math and the 2nd & 3rd grade teachers are furious at the 1st grade teacher for "creating" problems for them)
- the potential loss of high test scores if a student is accelerated through the grades in that school and "graduates" in less than the normal time
- reluctance to lose a year of student attendance (loss of ADA money for public schools, or tuition for private schools)
- general administrative rigidity ("If we make an exception for your child then we'll be besieged by parents who want special treatment for their children!") (Kauffman, n.p.)

SAVINGS BENEFITS

Accelerating students through the education system provides savings to parents or their child when proceeding with postsecondary education. The AP program is a curriculum in the United States sponsored by the College Board which offers standardized courses to high school students that are generally recognized to be equivalent to undergraduate courses in college.

Some colleges use AP test scores to exempt students from introductory coursework, others use them to place students in higher designated courses, and some do both. A high mark in these AP courses, while in senior high school, enables the student to skip a portion of their early college/university coursework thereby reducing the number of courses leading to graduation. A similar benefit is available through the International Baccalaureate (IB) program which is accepted at universities in over 115 countries.

Accelerating students also provides school districts with significant budgetary savings. Recall in our regional study how almost 17 percent of students were retained at least one additional year prior to grade ten. The majority of these retentions were simply the result of being born in the wrong months near the end of the school registration window. These students then require eleven years in the K–9 school program costing the school system approximately 1.5 percent averaged annually.

In addition to these students, who were declared sufficiently weak to justify retention, many others progressed with the additional assistance of remediation. Costs associated with assisting these students are not documented; however, experience demonstrated that many schools in the district were staffed with remedial services for these students.

Presumably, there is a natural distribution of talent; however, only approximately 1 percent of students were accelerated: a difference of almost 16 percent retained over the ten-year period (K–9). The savings averaged over this same period would be approximately 1.5 percent annually. In other words, improving the education of many students would actually require less funding, a rare phenomenon in education wherein requests for additional funding is a constant.

A critical point in this chapter is whether the school system is equally focused on the needs of the gifted students as it is with those struggling to maintain an adequate pace in their learning. Clearly, the research indicates how the *moral imperative* for dealing with weak students overrides the educational programming for the gifted.

KEY POINTS

- Student retentions were seventeen times more than accelerations in Alberta.
- Student acceleration is infrequent across the United States.

- Absence of early grade standardized testing is a major reason for low acceleration.
- The one-room schoolhouse facilitated individualized teaching.
- Academically gifted students can acquire a year's learning within a few weeks.
- Enrichment is a poor substitute for accelerating academically gifted students.
- Accelerating students produces savings for both the family and school system.

Chapter 15

COVID-19

Our world's struggle with the COVID-19 pandemic impacts students unlike any other event in our generation. Pandemics frequented various populations since the turn of this century, but the spread throughout the world of COVID-19 alarmed all nations especially since we held a high level of confidence in our capacity to deal with the disease. Turmoil and turbulent emotions abounded around the globe, and education was similarly embroiled because achieving normal routine is a priority.

School closures escalated from the end of February 2020 and were followed by a gradual shift to remote learning. In March, full school closures across North America accelerated and the U.S. school system, excepting Montana and Wyoming, closed its doors by the end of April. A new age of remote learning across the school system became the norm.

During the summer of 2020, considerable public debate regarding possible reopening in September ensued, and a calling by teachers for "strikes" gained momentum after hearing that they would be part of the "experiment" in reopening schools. Teachers' paranoia ensued and access to schools remained elusive until after the U.S. election when calls for school reopening crested and teacher strikes became common in large U.S. cities.

Parents wanted a return to their routine without worrying about custodial care for their young children. Their need should not be confused with the term "baby-sitting" used by some choosing to denigrate the school system. Education is part of our culture's essential services and, unfortunately, a generation of students is risked negatively by this calamity.

Emotional concerns surfaced in all age groups during the pandemic period. Ohanian (2021) summarized how mental health-related emergency room cases increased 24 percent for ages five to eleven, and 31 percent for ages twelve to seventeen since the pandemic began. Mathematics test scores during this period of impersonal learning decreased by as much as 10 percent in year-over-year comparisons.

Generally, educators escaped the negative consequences experienced by many in the workplace where workers were laid-off or experiencing reduced hours with reduced pay. Working online with students was a mainstay in education insulating teachers from loss of salary. Generally, protection for safely working with students in classrooms was the issue.

As waves of the pandemic continued, salary and safety conflated providing an obstacle for politicians attempting to restore some normalcy for their communities. Teachers' strikes dominated the news media in early 2021. Antonucci (2021) expressed a perspective regarding the purpose for these strikes despite agreements and funding for protections which may have exposed the real reason for contractual disobedience:

> The teachers unions recognized this well before anyone else. They know a bargaining situation when they see one. That's why for the past 10 months various local and state unions have issued reopening requirements, while the national unions released guidelines and funding demands. As is usually the case, some demands are reasonable, others are not, and still others are bargaining chips to be discarded in exchange for something the unions actually want. (N.p.)

In 2021, as governments sought to restart their economies, teacher pay emerged as a polarizing condition across the United States.

Will (2021) similarly responded to the emerging crises with his reporting of this sudden shift:

> The pandemic began with people cheering teachers for pivoting so quickly to remote instruction, said David Labaree, a professor emeritus at the Stanford Graduate School of Education. But now, teachers are seen by a vocal segment of the public "not as the first responders, but more the people blocking the path to the classroom door."
>
> Across the country and throughout the pandemic, teachers' unions have been pushing for a more conservative approach to getting teachers and kids back in

buildings. In some places, their political maneuvering has escalated. Members of the Chicago teachers' union voted Sunday to collectively refuse to work in person, despite the districts' orders. (N.p.)

Teachers' strikes in San Francisco, Los Angeles, and New York followed despite increased funding for personal protection equipment; however, motivation for these strikes remained a confusing issue.

Recall our earlier chapter on teacher pay and where the United States, in particular, stood in relation to other countries. Previous to the pandemic, public attitudes for increased wages were well supported, but somewhat deflected by school closures in the late stages of the pandemic. Strikes, presumably triggered by COVID-19 health concerns, could provide impetus where increased salaries were an acceptable trade-off for having schools reopen.

In March 2021, the potential for normalcy to resume schooling experienced a setback because of information regarding COVID variants. Whereas the initial North American strain was most serious for the elderly, variants transported to North America placed younger people at a higher risk (https://www.wsws.org/en/articles/2021/03/13/chic-m13.html). In February, according to the Illinois Health Department, schools became the single largest source of COVID-19 transmission as explained by their representative:

> That's what I'm trying to point out, that there is a lot of evidence that shows kids are maybe at higher relative risk than the previous strain here was, and a lot of the notions that kids are completely immune, or virtually immune, as they used to say, some of the pro-herd or natural infection herd immunity advocates used to say, is terribly dangerous. Kids need to mask and schools need to be ventilated. We cannot assume that simply going back to school, the kids will be safe, even if community transmission is dropping or low, and it's not dropping anymore. (N.p.)

As winter in 2021 changed to spring, many citizens, beginning with the elderly, are receiving vaccinations which should reduce infections. The impact of variants on young people in our school system remains an unknown as is the issue of whether current vaccines will be sufficient to deal with future variants.

Technology is a significant factor for overcoming concerns with this infectious virus, and how this mode of learning impacts education when the virus is contained is a major issue. Chaos creates conditions for change and the education system will surely experience many forces pulling in different directions. Crisis events frequently stir action, and, hopefully, policymakers will see an opportunity to address some of the issues presented in this book.

References

Alexander, K. L., Entwisle, D. R. and Olson, L. S. "Schools, Achievement, and Inequality: A Seasonal Perspective." *Educational Evaluation and Policy Analysis*, Summer, Vol. 23, No. 2, 2001.

Anderson, C. "Media Violence Effects on Children, Adolescents and Young Adults." *Health Progress*, July–August, 2016. https://www.chausa.org/publications/health-progress/article/july-august-2016/media-violence-effects-on-children-adolescents-and-young-adults.

Antonucci, M. "Analysis: Teachers Unions Are Positioning to Negotiate How and When Schools Will Reopen. Money, Not Safety, Will Decide." *The 74*, January 12, 2021. https://www.the74million.org/article/analysis-the-teachers-unions-are-positioning-to-negotiate-how-and-when-schools-will-reopen-money-not-safety-will-decide/.

Argenti, Diana. "Require Kindergarteners to be 5 by Sept. 1." *San Francisco Chronicle*, August 12, 2010.

Bailey, S., Chaffey, G., Gross, M., MacLeod, B., Merrick, C. and Targett, R. *Educational Options: Acceleration*. Canberra, Australia: Department of Education, Science and Training, 2004.

Baker, A. "Many New York City Teachers Denied Tenure in Policy Shift." *The New York Times*, August 17, 2012.

Bamesberger, M. "Nebraska's Master's Degree Bonuses for Teachers May Need Reconfiguring." *Daily Nebraskan*, February 3, 2011.

Barber, M. and Mourshed, M. *How the World's Best-Performing School Systems Come Out on Top*. New York: McKinsey and Company, 2007.

Black, Conrad. "Public-Sector Unions are a Blight on Our Society." *National Post*, May 4, 2013.

Boaz, D. "Education and the Constitution." *Cato at Liberty* (blog), Cato Institute. May 1, 2006. https://www.cato.org/blog/education-constitution.

Buddin, R. and Zamarro, G. "Teacher Qualifications and Student Achievement in Urban Elementary Schools." *Journal of Urban Economics*, Vol. 66, No. 2, September 2009.

Caumont, A. "More of Today's Single Mothers Have Never Been Married." Pew Research Center, August 16, 2013. https://www.pewresearch.org/fact-tank/2013/08/16/more-of-todays-single-mothers-have-never-been-married/#:~:text=By%202011%2C%20the%20share%20of,non%2Dmarital%20births%20and%20divorce.

Colangelo, N., Assouline, S. and Gross, M. U. M. *A Nation Deceived: How Schools Hold Back America's Brightest Students* (Vol. 1). Iowa City: University of Iowa.

Coughlan, S. "Teachers 'Give Higher Marks to Girls,'" *BBC News*, March 5, 2015. https://www.bbc.com/news/education-31751672.

Cummon, N. "Gender Differences in Individual Variation in Academic Grades Fail to Fit Expected Patterns for STEM." *Nature Communications*, Vol. 9, No. 3777, 2018. DOI: 10.1038/s41467-018-06292-010.1038/s41467-018-06292-0.

Dillon, S. "Teacher Grades: Pass or Be Fired." *The New York Times*, June 27, 2011.

Drolet, D. "Minding the Gender Gap." *AU University Affairs*, September 10, 2007.

Dueck, J. *Gender Fairness in Today's School*. Lanham, MD: Rowman & Littlefield Publishers, 2017.

Fullan, M. *The Moral Imperative of School Leadership*. Thousand Oaks, CA: Corwin Press, 2003.

Fullan, M. *Leadership and Sustainability: System Thinkers in Action*. Thousand Oaks, CA: Sage Publications, 2005.

Fullan, M. "Positive Pressure." *Springer International Handbooks of Education*, Vol. 23, No. 1, 119–130, 2009.

Gagne, F. "From Noncompetence to Exceptional Talent: Exploring the Range of Academic Achievement within and between Grade Levels." *Gifted Child Quarterly*, Vol. 49, No. 2, 139, 2005.

Gladwell, M. *Outliers*. New York: Little, Brown and Company, 2008.

Goe, L. and Stickler, L. M. "Teacher Quality and Student Achievement: Making the Most of Recent Research." *TQ Research and Policy Brief*, 2008. https://files.eric.ed.gov/fulltext/ED520769.pdf.

Golston, W. A. "Parents, Government, and Children: Authority Over Education in the Liberal Democratic State." *Nomos*, Vol. 44, 211–233, 2003. https://www.jstor.org/stable/2422007.6.

Gonzalez, J. "Kindergarten Redshirting: How Kids Feel About It Later in Life." *Cult of Pedagogy*, April 24, 2016. https://www.cultofpedagogy.com/academic-redshirting/.

Gorman, L. "Good Teachers Raise Student Achievement." *The Digest* (a publication by the National Bureau of Economic Research), No. 8, August 2005. https://www.nber.org/digest/aug05/good-teachers-raise-student-achievement.

Gramlich, J. "What the Data Says (and Doesn't Say) About Crime in the United States." Pew Research Center, November 20, 2020. https://www.pewresearch.org/fact-tank/2020/11/20/facts-about-crime-in-the-u-s/.

Grant, T. "The Great Decline: 60 Years of Religion in One Graph." Religion News Service, January 27, 2014. https://religionnews.com/2014/01/27/great-decline-religion-united-states-one-graph/.

Greene, J. P. *Education Myths: What Special Interest Groups Want You to Believe About Our Schools—And Why It Isn't So.* Lanham, MD: Rowman & Littlefield, 2005.

The Guardian. "How Does Birth Month Affect Your Child's Future? Find the Results Here." Datablog (blog), *The Guardian*, November 1, 2011. https://www.theguardian.com/news/datablog/2011/nov/01/birth-month-affects-results-well-being#:~:text=The%20birth%20month%20of%20young,of%20Fiscal%20Studies%20(IFS).&text=The%20results%20also%20show%20that,likely%20to%20attend%20top%20universities.

Hanushek, E. et al. "The Market for Teacher Quality." National Bureau of Economic Research, February 2005. https://www.nber.org/papers/w11154.

Hanushek, E., Widerhold, S. and Piopiunik, M. "Do Smarter Teachers Make Smarter Kids?" *Education Next*, Vol. 19, No. 2, February 20, 2019. https://www.educationnext.org/do-smarter-teachers-make-smarter-students-international-evidence-cognitive-skills-performance/.

Harlen, W. "A Systematic Review of the Evidence of the Impact on Students, Teachers and the Curriculum of the Process of Using Assessment by Teachers for Summative Purposes." Research Evidence in Education Library. London: EPPI-Centre, Social Science Research Unit, Institute of Education, University of London, 2004.

Harris, D. N. and Sass, T. R. "What Makes for a Good Teacher and Who Can Tell?" *Calder*, the Urban Institute, September 2009. https://www.researchgate.net/publication/255601291_What_Makes_for_a_Good_Teacher_and_Who_Can_Tell.

Heasley, S. "Special Education Enrollment Trends Upward." *Disability Scoop*, June 5, 2018. https://www.disabilityscoop.com/2018/06/05/special-ed-enrollment-upward/25150/.

Hilliard, J. "The Influence of Social Media on Teen Drug Use." Addiction Center, July 16, 2019. https://www.addictioncenter.com/community/social-media-teen-drug-use/.

Howell, W., West, M. and Peterson, P. "The Public Weighs in on School Reform." *EducationNext*, Fall, 2011.

Huggins, G. "Summer Learning Can be a Game Changer." *Education Week*, January 15, 2013.

Hughes-Jones, D., Alexander, C., Rudo, Z., Pan, D. and Vaden-Kiernan, M. *Teacher Resources and Student Achievement in High-Need Schools Research Report*. Southwest Educational Development Laboratory, January 2006. https://files.eric.ed.gov/fulltext/ED593897.pdf.

Jensen, B. and Reichl, J. *Better Teacher Appraisal and Feedback: Improving Performance*. Melbourne: Grattan Institute, 2011.

Jha, A. "Childhood Stimulation Key to Brain Development, Study Finds." *The Guardian*, October 14, 2012. https://www.theguardian.com/science/2012/oct/14/childhood-stimulation-key-brain-development.

Jones, J. "Episode 42: Kindergarten Redshirting." *The Cult of Pedagogy* (podcast), n.d. https://www.cultofpedagogy.com/episode-42/.

Juel, C., Biancarosa, G., Coker, D. and Deffes. R. "Walking with Rosie: A Cautionary Tale of Early Reading Instruction." *Educational Leadership*, Vol. 60, 12–18, 2003.

Karis, K. "Reason for Gender Gap in Universities Debated." *The Globe and Mail*, January 6, 2011. https://www.theglobeandmail.com/news/national/time-to-lead/reason-for-gender-gap-in-universities-debated/article560781/.

Kris, D. "Why Preschool is the 'Most Important Year' in a Child's Development." *MindShift*, published by KQED, September 15, 2017. https://www.kqed.org/mindshift/49205/why-preschool-is-the-most-important-year-in-a-childs-development.

Knowles, T. "The Trouble with Teacher Tenure: We Can't Make Progress if Bad Teachers Have Jobs for Life." *PREAL Blog* (blog), Inter-American Dialogue. June 18, 2010. https://www.thedialogue.org/blogs/2010/06/teacher-tenure/.

Koedel, C. "Grade Inflation for Education Majors and Low Standards for Teachers." *American Enterprise Institute*, No. 7, August 2011.

Kretschmann, J., Vock, M. and Lüdtke, O. "Acceleration in Elementary School: Using Propensity Score Matching to Estimate the Effects on Academic Achievement." *Journal of Educational Psychology*, Vol. 106, 1080–1095. DOI: 10.1037/a0036631, 2014.

Kyl, J. "John Kyl Quotes." *BrainyQuote*, n.d. https://www.brainyquote.com/quotes/jon_kyl_524669.

Lafee, S. "Student Evaluating Teachers." *School Administrator*, Vol. 71, No. 3, 17–25, March 2014. https://www.aasa.org/content.aspx?id=32692.

Lammam, C., Palacios, M., Ren, F. and Clemens, J. "Comparing Government and Private Sector Compensation in Quebec." The Fraser Institute, February 2015. https://www.fraserinstitute.org/sites/default/files/comparing-government-and-private-sector-compensation-in-QC.pdf.

Lee, S. Y., Olszewski-Kubilius, P. and Thomson, D. T. "Academically Gifted Students Perceived Interpersonal Competence and Peer Relationships." *Gifted Child Quarterly*, Vol. 56, 90–104, 2012.

Lewin, T. "School Chief Dismisses 241 Teachers in Washington." *New York Times*, July 23, 2010. https://www.nytimes.com/2010/07/24/education/24teachers.html.

Little, P. "Supporting Student Outcomes Through Expanded Learning Opportunities." Harvard Family Research Project, February 11, 2009.

Livingston, G. "Stay-at-home Moms and Dads Account for about One-in-five U.S. Parents." Pew Research Center, September 24, 2018. https://www.pewresearch.org/fact-tank/2018/09/24/stay-at-home-moms-and-dads-account-for-about-one-in-five-u-s-parents/.

Livingston, G. and Parker, K. "Chapter 1: Living Arrangements and Father Involvement" in *A Tale of Two Fathers*. Pew Research Center, June 15, 2011. https://www.pewresearch.org/social-trends/2011/06/15/chapter-1-living-arrangements-and-father-involvement/.

Lopez, M. and Gonzalez-Barrera, A. "Women's College Enrollment Gains Leave Men Behind." Pew Research Center, March 6, 2014. https://www.pewresearch.org/fact-tank/2014/03/06/womens-college-enrollment-gains-leave-men-behind/.

Lubinski, D., Webb, R. M., Morelock, M. J. and Benbow. C. "Top 1 in 10,000: A 10-Year Follow-Up of the Profoundly Gifted." *Journal of Applied Psychology*, Vol. 86, No. 4, 2001.

Marcus, J. "Why Men Are the New College Minority." *The Atlantic*, August 8th, 2017. https://www.theatlantic.com/education/archive/2017/08/why-men-are-the-new-college-minority/536103/.

McCluskey, N. "Retiring General Counsel's Shocking Admission: The NEA is a Union!" *Cato at Liberty* (blog), CATO Institute, July 10, 2009. https://www.cato.org/blog/retiring-general-counsels-shocking-admission-nea-union.

McFall, C. "Barr Says 'Notion' of Separation of Church and State Misunderstood Because of 'Militant Secularists.'" *Fox News*, September 23, 2020. https://www.foxnews.com/politics/barr-says-notion-of-separation-of-church-and-state-is-misunderstood-because-of-militant-secularists.

McGuinn, P. "Ringing the Bell for K–12 Teacher Tenure Reform." Center for American Progress, February 2010. https://www.americanprogress.org/issues/education-k-12/reports/2010/02/09/7314/ringing-the-bell-for-k-12-teacher-tenure-reform/.

Martin, S. "Gender Gap Widens as Women Graduates Outpace the Men." *The Australian*, August 15, 2015.

Mellon, E. "HISD Moves Ahead on Dismissal Policy." *Houston Chronicle*, January 14, 2010.

Miller, B. M. *The Learning Season: The Untapped Power of Summer to Advance Student Achievement*. Nellie Mae Education Foundation, 2007. https://clalliance.org/wp-content/uploads/files/Learning_Season_ES.pdf.

Murnane, R., Reardon, S., Mbekeani, P. and Lamb, A. "Who Goes to Private School?" *Education Next*, Vol. 18, No. 4, July 17, 2018. https://www.educationnext.org/who-goes-private-school-long-term-enrollment-trends-family-income/.

Nir, S. "Reading At Some Private Schools Is Delayed." *New York Times*, February 15, 2011.

Ohanian, L. "Political Dysfunction and Teacher Unions are Keeping California Kids Out of School." *The Hill*, February 8, 2021. https://thehill.com/opinion/education/537792-political-dysfunction-and-teacher-unions-are-keeping-california-kids-out-of.

Olito, F. "How the Divorce Rate has Changed over the Last 150 Years." *Insider*, January 30th, 2019. https://www.insider.com/divorce-rate-changes-over-time-2019-1#in-the-60s-the-rate-slowly-started-to-climb-again-ending-the-decade-with-a-new-high-32-annual-divorces-for-every-1000-americans-9.

Orso, A. "Does Redshirting Actually Benefit Kids? Inside the Big Kindergarten Readiness Decision Parents Make." *The Philadelphia Inquirer*, August 15, 2018. https://www.inquirer.com/philly/news/academic-redshirting-kindergarten-experts-prek-enrollment-20180815.html.

Patrick, M., Schulenberg, J., O'malley, P. Johnston, L. and Bachman, J. "Adolescents' Reported Reasons for Alcohol and Marijuana Use as Predictors of Substance Use and Problems in Adulthood." *Journal of Studies on Alcohol and Drugs*, Vol. 72, No. 1, 106–116, 2011. DOI: 10.15288/jsad.2011.72.106.

Peterson, P., Howell, W. and West, M. "Teachers' Unions Have a Popularity Problem." *Wall Street Journal*, June 4, 2012.

Pew Research Center. "Canada's Changing Religious Landscape." June 27, 2013. https://www.pewforum.org/2013/06/27/canadas-changing-religious-landscape/.

Pew Research Center. "Chapter 4: Single Mothers" in *Breadwinner Moms*, Pew Research Center, May 29, 2013. https://www.pewresearch.org/social-trends/2013/05/29/chapter-4-single-mothers/.

Pratt, S. "What About Those Diploma Exams?" *The Edmonton Journal*, November 28, 2011. https://edmontonjournal.com/news/local-news/what-about-those-diploma-exams.

Prothero, A. "What Are School Vouchers and How Do They Work?" *Education Week*, January 26, 2017. https://www.edweek.org/policy-politics/what-are-school-vouchers-and-how-do-they-work/2017/01.

Quinn, D. and Polikoff, M. "Summer Learning Loss: What Is It, and What Can We Do About It?" Brookings, September 14, 2017. https://www.brookings.edu/research/summer-learning-loss-what-is-it-and-what-can-we-do-about-it/.

Ramos, B. "Breaking the Tradition of Summer Vacation to Raise Academic Achievement." Summary published by ERIC, 2011. https://eric.ed.gov/?id=EJ955832.

Ratcliffe, R. "The Gender Gap at Universities: Where are All the Men?" *The Guardian*, January 29, 2013.

Reeves, D. "Accountability Essentials: Identifying and Measuring Teaching Practices" in *Accountability for Learning: How Teachers and School Leaders Can Take Charge*. Alexandria, VA: Association for Supervision and Curriculum Development (ASCD), 2004. https://www.ascd.org/books/accountability-for-learning?chapter=accountability-essentials-identifying-and-measuring-teaching-practices.

Ristic, M. "6 Reasons Why Preschool is Good for Your Child." Novak Djokovic Foundation, January 17, 2016. https://novakdjokovicfoundation.org/6-reasons-why-preschool-is-good-for-your-child/.

Robinson, S. "Teacher Evaluation: Why It Matters and How We Can Do Better." *Frontline Education*, 2018.

Rocheleau, M. "On Campus, Women Outnumber Men More Than Ever." *Boston Globe*, March 28, 2016.

Rogers, K. B. *Re-Forming Gifted Education: How Parents and Teachers Can Match the Program to the Child*. Scottsdale, AZ: Great Potential Press, 2002.

Roza, M. and Miller, R. "Separation of Degrees: State-by-state Analysis of Teacher Compensation for Master's Degrees." Center on Reinventing Public Education, published by Center for American Progress, July 2009. https://cdn.americanprogress.org/wp-content/uploads/issues/2009/07/pdf/masters_degrees.pdf?_ga=2.46706791.1799196095.1598048798-1627250001.1598048798.

Russo, A. "Teachers Unions and the Common Core." *Education Next*, Vol. 15, No. 1, October 29, 2014. https://www.educationnext.org/teachers-unions-common-core/.

Samuels, C. "Delaying a Child's Starting Age for School a Tough Call for Parents." *Education Week*, August 29, 2017. https://www.edweek.org/teaching-learning/delaying-childs-starting-age-for-school-a-tough-call-for-parents/2017/08.

Sawchuk, S. "Teacher Evaluation: An Issue Overview." *Education Week*, September 3, 2015. https://www.edweek.org/teaching-learning/teacher-evaluation-an-issue-overview/2015/09.

Schrier, A. "Joe Biden's First Date Began the End of Girls' Sports." *The Wall Street Journal*, January 22, 2021. https://www.wsj.com/articles/joe-bidens-first-day-began-the-end-of-girls-sports-11611341066.

Schwartz, C. "Teachers' Perceptions of the Effectiveness of Academic Acceleration." Master's thesis, Marshall University, 2016.

Srikanth, A. "After Biden Reestablishes Transgender Protections, Montana Lawmakers Move to Restrict Participation in School Sports." *The Hill*, January 21, 2021. https://thehill.com/changing-america/enrichment/education/535274-after-biden-reestablishes-transgender-protections.

Stanescu, B. "Transgender Athletes Robbing Girls of the Chance to Win Girls' Sports. Let My Daughter Compete Fairly." *USA Today*, June 19, 2020. https://www.usatoday.com/story/opinion/2020/06/19/transgender-athletes-robbing-girls-chance-win-sports-column/4856486002/.

Stanton, G. "Does Faith Reduce Divorce Risk?" *Public Discourse*, published by The Witherspoon Institute, March 22, 2018. https://www.thepublicdiscourse.com/2018/03/20935/.

Stinson, S. "Labour's $4B Election Fund: Unions Free to Spend Compulsory Dues on Political Activities." *National Post*, January 24, 2015. https://nationalpost.com/news/politics/labours-4b-election-fund-unions-free-to-spend-compulsory-dues-on-political-activities.

Swiatek, M. and Lupkowski-Shoplik, A. https://www.semanticscholar.org/paper/An-Evaluation-of-the-Elementary-Student-Talent-by-Swiatek-Lupkowski-Shoplik/dfd724e6072c0555af1145935ccb1bf8375ad374, 2004.

Tatter, G. "Federal Judge Dismisses TEA Lawsuit Challenging TVAAS in Teacher Bonuses." *Chalkbeat Tennessee*, February 19, 2016. https://tn.chalkbeat.org/2016/2/19/21100522/federal-judge-dismisses-tea-lawsuit-challenging-tvaas-in-teacher-bonuses.

Tausz, R. "Biden's Trans Order Undoes Decades of Feminist Progress." *New York Post*, January 22, 2021. https://nypost.com/2021/01/22/bidens-trans-order-undoes-decades-of-feminist-progress/.

Turnitin. "A Letter to Your Principal: Cell Phones," n.d. https://www.rcboe.org/cms/lib/GA01903614/Centricity/Domain/2605/CellPhoneRevisionAssistant.pdf.

Tyler, E. and Tyler, J. "Achievement." National Association of Secondary School Principals (NASSP), March 2020. https://www.nassp.org/publication/principal-leadership/volume-20/principal-leadership-march-2020/teacher-evaluations-march-2020/.

UKEssays. "Should Teachers Get Tenure?" November 2018. https://www.ukessays.com/essays/education/should-teachers-get-tenure.php.

Walsh, M. "Transgender Issues at School a Subtext as High Court Weighs Sex-Bias Cases." *Education Week*, October 8, 2019. https://www.edweek.org/education/transgender-issues-at-school-a-subtext-as-high-court-weighs-sex-bias-cases/2019/10.

Wang, W. "The U.S. Divorce Rate Has Hit a 50-Year Low." Institute for Family Studies, November 10, 2020. https://ifstudies.org/blog/the-us-divorce-rate-has-hit-a-50-year-low.

Webber, C., Aitken, N., Lupart, J. and Scott, S. "The Alberta Student Assessment Study." *The Crown in Right of Alberta*, 2009. https://archive.org/stream/albertastudentas00webb/albertastudentas00webb_djvu.txt.

Weisberg, D., Sexton, S., Mulhern, J. and Keeling, D. "The Widget Effect." The New Teacher Project, June 8, 2009. https://tntp.org/publications/view/the-widget-effect-failure-to-act-on-differences-in-teacher-effectiveness.

Will, M. "Has the Public Turned On Teachers?" *Education Week*, January 25, 2021. https://www.edweek.org/teaching-learning/has-the-public-turned-on-teachers/2021/01.

Williams, S. *The Skeptic's Guide to Eternal Bliss.* New York: Grand Central Publishing, 2009.

Woods, M. "Making the Grade." *Queen's Journal*, September 19, 2008. https://www.queensjournal.ca/story/2008-09-19/features/making-the-grade/.

www.ingramcontent.com/pod-product-compliance
Lightning Source LLC
Chambersburg PA
CBHW051811230426
43672CB00012B/2692